PRAISE FOR *LEAD EVERY DAY*

"This book is a game changer for leaders who are serious about building high-performance organizations. The authors have masterfully combined decades of research and real-world experience into an actionable system that works at every level of leadership. The way they address talent, teams, and organizational excellence is brilliant and practical."

—Ken Kencel, President and CEO, Churchill Asset Management, LLC

"Finally, a leadership book that ignites the leader instead of exhausting one. *Lead Every Day* is a must-read for individuals who desire to masterfully leverage their leadership gifts and unlock their greatest potential. The book offers actionable steps for leaders to stay fueled, while harnessing the passions of those around them. After all, the leadership journey does not wait for others to empower. It begins within."

—Vanita Boswell, PhD, CEO, The VALO Group, and Executive Producer, Netflix Original Documentary *Rooting for Roona*

"I've had the pleasure of working with some of the best leadership teachers out there, but Mark and Randy break down the age-old mystery of leadership in the simplest, most effective way I've seen. Hugely beneficial to anyone looking to lead yourself and those around you better!"

-Aaron Witt, Founder, BuildWitt

"The most practical leadership guide I've encountered in over 25 years of leading."

—Bill Canady, Chairman and CEO, Arrowhead Engineered Products

"*Lead Every Day* is an uncertainty-tested playbook for real leadership—practical, no fluff, just a proven system to help you lead with clarity, build high-performing teams, and create an unstoppable culture of excellence. If you're serious about leadership, this book is your best choice."
—Alden Mills, Navy SEAL Platoon Commander,
Bestselling Author, and Founder, Be Unstoppable

"After serving more than 8,000 non-profit leaders, operational effectiveness is often sacrificed in the name of mission advancement. For sustained, elite performance, leaders must adopt an effective operating system, which is why *Lead Every Day* is the first book I recommend. It is exactly what leaders need—a systematic, daily approach to building exceptional organizations."
—Sadie Elliott, Training Director, Herzog Foundation

"In my 30-plus years of leading soldiers around the world, I have found many times a leader's experience can be their weakness if they do not evolve. Mark Miller and Randy Gravitt strip away the mystique and provide a clear and concise road map to become a better leader based on successes in the real world. This is a must-read for the new manager or seasoned C-suite executive."
—Colonel Glenn C. Schmick (retired), Army Advisor, Air
War College, and Ranger's Ridge Leadership Coach

LEAD
EVERY
DAY

LEAD EVERY DAY

Three Essential Disciplines to Unleash the Passion and Performance of Everyone Around You

MARK MILLER AND RANDY GRAVITT

Matt Holt Books
An Imprint of BenBella Books, Inc.
Dallas, TX

Matt Holt is an imprint of BenBella Books, Inc.
8080 N. Central Expressway
Suite 1700
Dallas, TX 75206
benbellabooks.com
Send feedback to feedback@benbellabooks.com

BenBella and *Matt Holt* are federally registered trademarks.

Printed in the United States of America
10 9 8 7 6 5 4 3 2 1

Library of Congress Control Number: 2025007642
ISBN 9781637747278 (hardcover)
ISBN 9781637747285 (electronic)

Editing by Katie Dickman
Copyediting by Michael Fedison
Proofreading by Lisa Story and Denise Pangia
Text design and composition by Aaron Edmiston
Cover design by Brigid Pearson
Printed by Versa Press

For our parents, teachers, coaches, supervisors, mentors, and friends who have shown us what it means to Lead Every Day.

CONTENTS

INTRODUCTION

Every action you take is a vote for the type of person you wish to become.
—James Clear

How did you learn to lead? If you're like most leaders, this is a complex question. Here's why: Chances are high you took a quite common path to leadership. You were likely good at something—selling something, making widgets, meeting your deadlines, hitting your quotas, or perhaps making good presentations to management. You were an individual contributor who distinguished yourself through personal excellence. Based on some version of this story, you were asked to move into leadership.

Now, here's the scoop: The person inviting you to assume a new role knew you weren't ready, but someone was needed; there was a problem to solve, an opportunity to seize, or an open position to fill. They were placing a bet you would do one of two things:

a. You would figure it out . . . this leadership thing, or
b. You would fail and be replaced.

Seeing the upside of the opportunity, you agreed and began your leadership journey. Our guess is that many of you received no formal training for your new assignment. Far too often, those who did receive training found it to be limited, theoretical, or technical in nature. For example, "Here's our corporate Performance

Management System. This is where you record team member goals and performance reviews." Tragically, many of you were never taught *how* to help team members set those goals or conduct a productive performance conversation, much less how to coach people along the way to increase their odds of success.

Undaunted, many of you forged ahead allowing the school of hard knocks to be your guide. Many of you read a book or two or ten, attended a random conference, and maybe even had a mentor along the way. If you were fortunate, you may have had a good supervisor at some point who provided some much-needed coaching. But honestly, when you look at all these activities in their totality, your tenacity sustained you as much as your growing skill set. Your leadership development was not strategic—it was sporadic at best.

You obviously didn't crash and burn too often, or the missteps you did experience were not career ending, or you probably wouldn't be reading this book. Very slowly, perhaps over many years, you began to understand the essence of leadership in action. You began to grow in competence and confidence. Your organization won their bet; you figured out how to lead. Congratulations!

WHO THIS BOOK WAS WRITTEN FOR

Here's the question we* want you to wrestle with from the outset of our time together:

"How's your leadership journey progressing?"

Are you fulfilled in your role or floundering? Energized or

---

* Throughout the book, we will use the pronoun "we" to represent Mark and Randy's collective thoughts or experiences. As coauthors, we were not comfortable representing our ideas in the first person. Nor could we figure out how to indicate who was speaking at any given point. "This is Randy . . ." and "This is Mark . . ." felt very clunky.

exhausted? Crushing it or being crushed? Are you happy with your present level of achievement and effectiveness? Are you confident regarding the next steps on your leadership journey? Do you feel you still have things to learn? Do you want to do more?

Regardless of your responses to these questions, this book is for you!

Wait. I'm not sure that makes sense. Let me get this straight: Even without knowing my answers to any of your questions, you think this book is for me? So, that must mean this book is for every leader. Right?

Almost.

A wide array of leaders from all levels of experience and responsibility could provide vastly different answers to the questions above. Based on any of those responses, yes, this book would still be helpful for them. However, there is one additional consideration. Do you fit the following profile?

This book is for leaders who:

- Believe they can make a difference in their world.
- Care deeply about personal excellence.
- Are energized by producing tangible results.

Assuming these attributes describe you, we're excited to work alongside you and help you Lead Every Day.

THE PROMISE OF THIS BOOK

The promise of the book is simple: We will show you how to unleash the passion and performance of everyone around you.

We want your results to exceed your wildest expectations—whatever you choose: sales; profits; customer satisfaction; building a strong, perhaps industry-leading brand; or anything else. If you decide what you are trying to accomplish and then embrace the disciplines contained in the following pages, your success is inevitable.

If you serve in the not-for-profit arena, your success metrics will likely look different from those in the marketplace, but they are no less significant. Just imagine whatever good you are attempting to do in the world multiplied by a factor of 10 or 20 or 50. What would the world look like if you were able to increase your impact exponentially? You can!

We invite you to join us on a lifelong journey to learn, grow, and practice three primary disciplines that form the core of the Lead Every Day Operating System.

- Become a Better Leader
- Improve Team Performance
- Strengthen Your Organization

Our hopes and dreams for *you* and leaders around the world are straightforward: We want *you* to know what you need *to do* to lead well. We have little patience with, or use for, theories about leadership. Our focus is the "Practice of Leadership."

We've been serving leaders for decades. The training, coaching, consulting, keynote talks, podcasts, social media posts, LinkedIn articles, and all the resources we've produced, including this book, have one through line:

You practice your way to high performance.

"Yes, but how?" is the most often-asked question we've received over the last four decades. This is *the* question as we consider all the content we'll share in the pages that follow. We created this book to help you begin to answer this question.

The **Practice!** assignments throughout the text will transform this book from a nice-to-read into the Lead Every Day Operating System mentioned previously. When the OS is in place, sustained high performance will be within your reach.

Once you understand and begin to apply the ideas we are presenting, you'll become more proficient and comfortable creating your own ideas for action. If you want a visual here, think of musicians who can improvise, leaving the sheet music behind to create something special. This is only possible because they have mastered the key disciplines of their art form. Be patient; you'll learn to do the same.

Becoming a great leader isn't about having some rare natural talent—it's about putting in the *right* kind of work. Psychologist K. Anders Ericsson is an internationally recognized researcher in the field of high performance. He has studied experts across numerous domains, including medicine, music, chess, sports, and more. His research shows that expertise isn't a gift; it's earned through deliberate practice. This kind of practice isn't found in mindless repetition—it's about setting clear goals, constantly pushing yourself beyond your current abilities, and using feedback to fuel your improvement. Leaders, like athletes or musicians, can elevate their skills by focusing on areas that challenge them. With consistent effort, feedback, and a commitment to growth, anyone can develop into a truly exceptional leader.[1]

The story of the Polgár sisters brings this to life. Their parents wanted their children to be exceptional chess players. They didn't want to rely on talent alone—they created a plan of focused, intentional training from an early age. Through countless hours of deliberate practice, all three sisters became some of the best chess players in the world. Judit, the youngest, became a grand master by age 15. Their success proves that with the right approach, mastery is within reach—whether it's in chess or leadership.[2]

In this book we will show you how to practice your way to high performance. We have invested the majority of our adult lives working to make the complexities of leadership simple, approachable, and applicable.

That is what you are about to encounter: the simple truth about some life-changing leadership disciplines and best practices. As James Clear writes in *Atomic Habits*, "Every action you take is a vote for the type of person you wish to become."[3] Nowhere is this truer than in leadership.

OUR RESEARCH METHODOLOGY

When we read leadership books, we're always interested in the foundation for the work. Said another way, we are always asking ourselves, "What is their source of truth?"

"Thought leadership" comes in several forms. In one camp, the conclusions and recommendations the authors make are based exclusively on their own experiences. Sometimes, their content is solid and actually works. However, much of what you'll find in this world is not universally true or transferable. The ideas worked for the author in a unique and specific circumstance.

There is another camp of thought leaders comprised of those in academia or with a strong research bias. These are brilliant minds, and some of our dearest friends are part of this group. They know the "truth" based on their research and the study of others. Again, this approach is very thoughtful but not always approachable and practical in the real world.

For our work over the last several decades, we have chosen to bring the practitioner's view and the research together.

We have been leading for a long time. We have led teams and helped build large and successful organizations. We also have the benefit of decades of research in search of the answer to a simple question: What is universally true about this topic (High Perfomance Teams, engagement, culture, leadership effectiveness, etc.)? Our research has covered the gamut. We've conducted 12 independent projects over the last 25 years. We studied the world's best teams, organizations with thriving cultures and those capable of extraordinary levels of execution, and much more. This book includes many of the insights we gleaned along the way. We know many of you are interested in the research. Every project had its own unique research design. We've typically employed a combination of qualitative and quantitative methods. Numerous projects have included thousands of participants. For our work on organizational culture, we interviewed or surveyed over 6,000 leaders and individual contributors from seven countries; for the talent work, we included over 7,000 US-based individual contributors; for the latest leadership survey, we included over 4,000 participants from five countries.

Over the years, our partners have included brilliant minds from Stanford University and several of the world's leading consulting firms. We have conducted multimillion-dollar projects on improving leadership effectiveness, building High Performance Teams, creating a leadership culture, designing organizational culture, attracting and keeping Top Talent, improving engagement, and creating a culture known for elite levels of execution and more.

We have not only researched these topics; we have shared our findings with countless organizations—for-profits, not-for-profits, schools, churches, government agencies, agricultural businesses, hospitals, professional sports teams, restaurants—and now make annual visits to the Joint Forces War College to serve senior military leaders from more than 40 countries. We share with them some of the practices in this book. Our books are currently in 25 translations with more than one million copies in print.

We've worked with hundreds of organizations over the last decade helping them practice their way to high performance. We've given more than a thousand keynotes and hosted hundreds of workshops around the world. We have consulted with multibillion-dollar companies, served hundreds of small to mid-sized organizations, and our podcast is now serving leaders in over 150 countries. We've also coached more than 1,500 individual leaders along the way. The success we've seen when our content is deployed anywhere in the world bolsters our confidence and our passion to share these truths with you.

Our research, exposure to global leaders, and firsthand experience leading and building teams and organizations have proven one thing to be true over and over: Leaders do have the power to change their world, and we can show you how.

Oh, a quick disclaimer is in order while you're reading this introduction: Because our core belief is that you practice your way to high performance, we need to say a word about what *doesn't* work. Yes, we've had our fair share of clients who were not successful. We thought we should give you a heads-up. Here's the bottom line:

No practice, no performance.

You cannot wish or hope your way to the results you desire. You must do the work.

WHAT'S NEXT?

We wrote this book for you. We both wish we had a resource like this decades ago. If you read, apply, and ultimately teach the disciplines and best practices contained on the following pages, we promise you'll see amazing results.

Leadership is fundamentally a skill set that with practice becomes a mindset. What you do through conscious effort in the beginning, with practice, will become your reflexive response. You will move from performing the tasks of leadership to being a leader. We believe you can do it, or we wouldn't have invested the time to write this book for you.

The question is not can you do it, but will you choose to invest yourself fully in the Practice of Leadership? Are you willing to Lead Every Day? For your team, your organization, your family, your community, and your legacy—will you? What's next is up to you.

Let's do something great together.

UPDATE YOUR OPERATING SYSTEM

When you're ready, the right operating system will appear in your life.
—Guy Kawasaki

D o you remember your first cell phone? We're guessing you do. In the early days of cellular technology, there was something cool about connecting with people wirelessly. Today, what most people once thought to be a miracle is now mundane. This is an interesting response to a staggering increase in capability. As the pace of technology has continued to accelerate, our sense of wonder has diminished.

Today, there are almost two million apps in Apple's App Store and almost three million on Google Play Store[1] (we've even created a Lead Every Day app). There have been many advances in technology over the years that have contributed to this explosion of functionality—improved battery life, faster networks, interactive displays, and more. Yes, our phones can still make calls, but they can do so much more. The enabler for all these innovations to work together, the wizard behind the curtain, is the Operating System (OS).

WHAT IS AN OPERATING SYSTEM?

Let's begin with a simple definition:

> **An Operating System is a predetermined set of instructions that enables higher operating speed, greater efficiency, and improved performance.**

Just imagine how good it would be if you had an OS enabling you to produce more and better results faster with less effort.

Okay, at this point, some of you have a question: "*How can you promise higher speed, greater efficiency, and improved performance?*" It's an easy promise to make because the Lead Every Day Operating System will help you do the following.

Focus Attention. There are so many things warring for a leader's attention. We've devoted an entire chapter to how to best respond to the "quicksand" you confront on a daily basis. In the midst of the pandemonium we often encounter, where do the best leaders focus their attention? We'll answer this question in greater detail in the pages to follow, but to provide you with a 50,000-foot view, the best leaders are concerned with three things. How to:

- Become a Better Leader
- Improve Team Performance
- Strengthen Your Organization

If you focus on these disciplines, your impact will grow exponentially. The Lead Every Day OS will be your guide to new levels of focus and achievement.

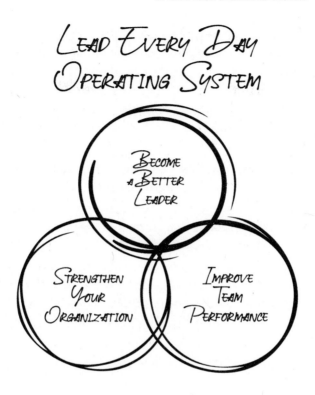

Leverage Knowledge. When the Operating System in your phone was developed, it was programmed with the latest information. From time to time, there is an update available with more current information, and often, new features as well. To enjoy these additional benefits, you must choose to participate–you must update your phone. If you do not, you forfeit what is within your reach.

When you want to go somewhere you may not have been before, you can use the GPS in your phone, or you can choose to pull that paper map out of your glove box your dad left in there two decades ago. The map *might* get you to your destination, but our money is on GPS.

The information we've included in the Lead Every Day OS is built on timeless principles, extensive (and expensive) global research, and rigorous real-world experience. The ideas you'll be exposed to will work in any industry regardless of the size of your organization. And, because the content is principle-based, it will work anywhere in the world.

Inform Sequencing. When you were very young, you began to learn about the vast topic of mathematics. In the beginning, you were not aware of the expansiveness of the subject. All you knew is that people you trusted, and in many cases admired, began to teach you about numbers. When you first started, this may have seemed like a random activity—like learning your colors, or how to tell the difference between a monkey and a cat. However, over time, you began to see the utility of what you had learned; numbers could be added and subtracted. In a moment of clarity, the value of numbers moved from the abstract to the concrete.

Later, on your learning journey, someone explained the concept of multiplication and division, then fractions . . . wow! Numbers are powerful. Yes, they are. And, if you stayed on course, you learned about algebra, geometry, trigonometry, and even calculus. The value and applicability of the numbers you learned as a child increased exponentially as you progressed through a proper sequence of instruction. The same concept is true with leadership.

When leaders do not understand the basics of leadership, teams, or organizational success, they often compound their challenges rather than resolve them. As an example, a leader who cannot Embody a Leader's Heart will always struggle with improving team performance. Our Operating System will prepare you with the necessary skills in an order that will help you learn and apply them more easily.

Improve Performance. A good Operating System provides the information you need to make better choices. If you are informed such that you make better choices, and in turn, take smarter actions, your performance will improve. Let's go back to the GPS example we mentioned a few paragraphs back. When you are confronted with two routes to your desired destination and one is clogged by an accident, choose the faster, less congested route, and you will spend less time in the car. The Lead Every Day OS will give you the fastest route to your destination. The practices we are advocating have made organizations hundreds of millions, even billions, of dollars over the years. When you activate the content, you will lead at a higher level, your team's performance will improve, and your organization will become stronger.

RETURN ON LEADERSHIP

You may be reading this and asking yourself, *Why do I need an operating system?* Fantastic question! Let's be clear, you do have one. Unfortunately, it may be a compilation of conventional wisdom, old wives' tales, and a few random best practices, with a modicum of hard-won wisdom developed over the years. This piecemeal approach is inadequate to maximize your leadership in our dynamic world. If you want to maximize your return on leadership, you need an updated and proven Operating System!

We're guessing you didn't buy your phone because of the Operating System. You bought a new phone for the additional features and benefits. What many do not fully appreciate is that the new features your phone is capable of after an update are a direct reflection of the Operating System. The OS is the enabler of the benefits you seek. The OS we're offering you will enable you to unleash the passion and performance of everyone around you.

What could a long-term commitment to the Lead Every Day OS look like? Consider the following example from one of our clients.

After embracing the Lead Every Day OS for more than a decade, Arrow Exterminators quadrupled their business from $100 million to over $400 million in revenue, growing from 1,000 team members to over 3,400 with locations all over the United States. Their simple strategy has been to invest in their leaders, while challenging them to grow the business by 10% each year. The company has met their goal of double-digit growth for 13 consecutive years! Arrow's focus on leadership, talent, alignment, engagement, and execution (more on all these topics later in the book) has led to them becoming one of the most successful and best companies to work for you'll find anywhere.

Beyond the success of our clients like Arrow and scores of others, there's another reason we're so confident in the Lead Every Day OS—the success of Chick-fil-A (CFA) over the years. You'll see numerous "chicken" examples throughout the pages that follow. We worked to limit the number, but it was difficult. Mark invested almost 45 years of his life at the company and Randy has trained more than 20,000 Chick-fil-A leaders. Our team has also coached hundreds of the company's leaders over the last decade.

Now, we are quick to add, we are not claiming the credit for the organization's meteoric rise. There are many factors that even the casual observer would identify as critical elements in their success, starting with local ownership. Chick-fil-A Operators are extremely talented independent businesspeople who have attracted amazing team members. The company has a savvy real estate team, outstanding men and women in product development, world-class IT and marketing, and thousands of other dedicated staff members whose primary role is to make the restaurant Operators successful. The organization has created an extraordinary recipe for success.

In the midst of all of this, you can find Chick-fil-A's deep-seated belief and understanding that everything rises and falls on leadership. The company invested tens of millions of dollars in time, energy, research, consultants, best-practice visits, and testing to discover the principles and practices we will outline in the following pages. The ideas in this book have been adopted voluntarily by many of the company's independent Operators. They are an ongoing testimony to the fact that the ideas in this book work.

Every leader needs a state-of-the-art Operating System! But we'll say it again: The goal is *not* to have a new Operating System. It is to enable you to unleash the passion and performance of everyone around you. As a result, your organization will consistently produce results that exceed your expectations.

HOW ARE YOU DOING . . . REALLY?

We know if you're reading this book, you are a leader who takes your responsibilities seriously. We also assume you are already doing many things well. Congratulations! However, in the spirit of continuous improvement and stewardship, we believe you are open to "upgrading" your Operating System.

To help you gain a sense of where your greatest opportunities may lie, we've created a quick diagnostic tool. Think of this as a scan of your hard drive.

You know how these things work. Be honest, and don't over-think it. If you are torn between two ratings, choose the lower one. Our research has discovered that our optimism as a leader, while essential, doesn't help us when we're attempting to provide an objective self-analysis. We recommend just writing your response in the space provided.

The Lead Every Day Operating System Assessment

Indicate your *agreement* with each of the following statements using a 5-point scale: 1 = Strongly Disagree, 5 = Strongly Agree.

		Your Score
1.	Those searching for a leadership role model need look no further—just follow my example.	
2.	I have a written plan for my personal and professional development that I monitor and update regularly.	
3.	Clarity is king within our team/organization.	
4.	Everyone is crystal clear on our aspirations (e.g., mission, vision, purpose, values, etc.) and their individual success metrics.	
5.	My leadership is not encumbered by busyness, distractions, complexity, fatigue, fear, or aimlessness.	
6.	I consistently lead to my full potential.	
7.	We consistently attract the best people in our industry to join our team/organization.	
8.	We are an organization predominantly staffed with "A Players."	
9.	All of our organization's teams are highly effective.	
10.	Our teams consistently produce ever-improving results.	
11.	The women and men on our teams care deeply about each other as people, not just as coworkers.	
12.	The people on our teams spend time with each other outside of the workplace.	
13.	We have an ample supply of highly skilled leaders to meet the organization's current demands.	

14.	We have a pipeline of emerging leaders who will be ready to lead us into the future.	
15.	Our organization's culture is strong, performance-enhancing, and life-giving.	
16.	Everyone in the organization is actively working to help us make our cultural aspirations a reality (e.g., mission, vision, purpose, values, etc.).	
17.	All of our employees care deeply about their work, their coworkers, our customers, and the organization.	
18.	We have established an ongoing system with clear metrics to monitor the engagement of our employees.	
19.	Our people consciously and consistently strive to do the right thing, the right way, every time.	
20.	Our organization is known for elite levels of execution.	
	Your Score	

You know the drill. Add up your scores. We know your next question—what is a good score? Well, the maximum score is 100. But don't fixate on your score. We'd like to ask you a few questions:

- How do you *feel* about the scores?
- What surprised you?
- Which scores would you like to improve?
- Do you believe your scores represent what you and your organization are capable of?

We obviously don't know how you responded to any of the statements above or our summary questions, but there are a few things we feel confident concluding.

First, regardless of your scores, you can improve. You must start where you are but you do not have to stay there. The Lead Every Day Operating System will guide your journey.

Next, based on our two most recent global surveys with more than 10,000 participants, we know there is typically a gap between what leaders and those who report to them think. This gap tends to hover around 30 points![2, 3] Yes, 30 points. We chalk up this discrepancy to two primary factors: (1) Leaders are by nature an optimistic lot and (2) far too many leaders are out of touch with those they lead. We share this so you will proceed with caution, particularly if you scored yourself extremely high on any of the statements above.

Our final conclusion: You and your organization are capable of much more than you presently believe.

If you want some sophisticated diagnostic analysis of your data, the first six questions are focused on you—**Becoming a Better Leader**. The next six are focused on your team—**Improving Team Performance**. The final eight questions are about your organization—**Strengthening Your Organization**. If you have a fire to put out in one of these areas, you may want to go to the corresponding part of the book first, or reference the Troubleshooting Guide on pages 265–266. As you attempt to address individual issues, always remember the disciplines are interdependent and, to improve in one area, it will often require focused effort beyond the specific problem at hand.

We suggest that you take this assessment *every six months* for the rest of your career. You can photocopy the one above or take the assessment for free at **https://leadeveryday.com/os-assessment** or scan this QR code:

ARE YOU READY?

While doing our homework on Operating Systems, we found this quote from Steve Jobs. We knew this is how we wanted to end this opening chapter.

"We've gone through the operating system and looked at everything and asked how can we simplify this and make it more powerful at the same time."[4]

This is exactly the process we embraced while writing this book.

We took our 75-plus years of real-world leadership experience, combined it with millions of dollars of research, and infused global best practices from leaders and organizations that consistently set the standard for performance. The result: the Lead Every Day Operating System. A system that is principle-based and field-tested. The ideas in this book work! If you adopt our Operating System, you will unleash the passion and performance of everyone around you.

When we saw our first smartphone, we said, "Wow!" The capabilities were breathtaking. The same can be true for your leadership. Are you ready to be amazed and inspired? You can accomplish more than you ever dreamed possible and literally change your world. We're going to show you how.

Begin downloading your new Lead Every Day Operating System and get ready to say, "Wow!"

LEAD EVERY DAY OPERATING SYSTEM

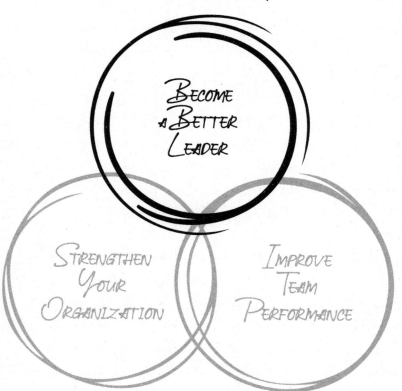

BECOME A BETTER LEADER

STRENGTHEN YOUR ORGANIZATION

IMPROVE TEAM PERFORMANCE

BECOME A BETTER LEADER

Everything rises and falls on leadership.
—John Maxwell

Why would you want to Become a Better Leader? Honestly, we don't know your deepest motives and it's not really our place to judge them. However, we hope your heart aches for the world to be better because of your brief time on this stage we call life. Every business, nonprofit organization, home, place of worship, school, and hospital can be a place of transformation . . . if they are well-led. We dream of a world well-led!

We also think you understand either intuitively or from experience that John Maxwell's above quote is true. Everything really does rise and fall on leadership. We just want to remind you of a few reasons why what you do matters—even more than you think.

Look at the following statistics and consider what they all have in common.

- In 1980, 40% of the world lived in extreme poverty; today, that number is 10%.[1]

- Worldwide, 186 nations (out of 196) have some social security for people with disabilities.[2]
- In 1900, 40% of children in the world died before the age of five; today, that number is 4%.[3]
- Worldwide, 90% of girls go to primary school (for boys, that number is 91%).[4]
- More than 80 countries have satellites circling the earth.[5]

What do every one of these accomplishments have in common? *Leadership.* We are quick to acknowledge there is far more to do in all the areas mentioned above and countless more opportunities for progress in countless arenas around the world. That is the point—the untapped potential that remains in the world, the opportunities to seize, suffering to be addressed, and value to be created. All of this is precisely why *your* life and *your* leadership matter. The things that need to happen in this world—the good that needs to be done, the injustices that need to be set right—none of this will happen without leadership.

HIGH PERFORMANCE BEGINS WITH YOU

Unapologetically, we have invested the vast majority of our professional careers helping leaders grow. No team or organization will outgrow their leaders. However, when leaders continue to learn and grow, the sky is the limit. Dreams once thought impossible can become the stepping stones for even more audacious accomplishments in the future. You are the key. Therefore, we'll begin our journey together exploring what is required for you to Become a Better Leader. This is the first discipline in the Lead Every Day Operating System.

To help you Become a Better Leader, we've identified three

primary strategies and some of their accompanying best practices for you to begin incorporating into your daily life. Here's a quick overview of what we'll cover in this section.

Learn the Fundamentals. What are the most pressing issues you are currently facing as a leader? Here are some of the usual suspects we hear all the time: turnover; profitability; engagement; sales; innovation, or the lack thereof; a shortage of leaders; and more. We have good news for you. The first step to tackle any of these issues, and whatever else is on your list, begins with the fundamentals of leadership. We have invested decades defining, validating, and refining the fundamentals we're going to help you develop. This first chapter is not necessarily the most important in the book, but it is foundational. Many of the challenges you'll face as you try to Improve Team Performance and Strengthen Your Organization have their root in a shortfall on one or more of the fundamentals. These five fundamentals will set you up for leadership success for the rest of your life.

Create Clarity. One of the greatest contributions leaders can make is to give the gift of clarity. Tragically, we see the absence of clarity virtually every week. This year alone, we've spoken to leaders from more than a thousand organizations. Unfortunately, confusion and ambiguity are the norm.

The absence of clarity would be funny if the consequences were not so catastrophic. This topic clearly falls into the "you can't make this stuff up" category. We've encountered multibillion-dollar organizations and hundreds of smaller ones who literally cannot agree on what they are trying to accomplish or what they value or even the key strategies they will pursue. The lack of clarity in most organizations is a silent threat lurking in the shadows that devours human and organizational potential.

We want to challenge and equip you to differentiate yourself as a leader. If your team knows their performance goals and key health indicators, all your teams have a clear charter, your meetings have documented Action Items, and your organization is clear on what matters most, you'll be among the elite organizations in the world. Oh, and before we're done, you'll also have a clear cultural aspiration and an agreed-upon definition of leadership. This is the power of the Lead Every Day Operating System in action.

Improve Your Effectiveness. We have been asked more than once about the most pressing issue leaders face around the world. This is a challenging question for many reasons. We acknowledge that all leadership is local. We also know that context matters. So does the health of the organization you serve. Our list of disclaimers could go on and on. However, having traveled, taught, interviewed, and surveyed leaders in dozens of countries around the world, we have no reservations to name lack of leadership effectiveness as Leadership Enemy Number One.

We look forward to going deeper with you on this critical topic. For now, we'll say that most leaders could lead at higher levels and have greater impact if it weren't for those things holding them back. Again, the list of impediments can be long and very personal. Common obstacles often include busyness, distractions, complexity, fear, fatigue, and more. We call the sum of these elements *quicksand*. We will help you escape.

We're thankful you are here, and we're excited about the impact you are going to have in your world and the world at large. The ripple effect of your life and leadership will be determined by your actions. Don't miss your moment!

LEARN THE FUNDAMENTALS

A journey of a thousand miles begins with the first step.
—Laozi

A few years ago, Randy was in spring training working with the coaches of the Pittsburgh Pirates organization. On the final day of camp, Randy happened to be on the field when he noticed the team working on rundowns for any time an opposing baserunner was caught between third base and home plate. When a baserunner is caught in a rundown, the game turns chaotic, unless . . . unless a defense understands the fundamentals of executing the play. Watching the practice, Randy recalled how he and his brother had practiced the same thing as kids back in elementary school, only they called it hotbox—a drill designed to train players on who would cover the bases and how to move in response to the baserunner's actions. He wondered why major leaguers would be practicing such a trivial drill.

Three days later, the Pirates started their season against the Cubs, and you guessed it. The game ended with a Cubs runner rounding third too aggressively. The Pirates were prepared, and the runner was trapped in a rundown and eventually tagged out. Game over. It turns out that whether you are a Little Leaguer or a Big Leaguer, the fundamentals are the same, and they win games!

Fundamentals are the governing principles or practices within a discipline. They are the building blocks of success. You can see this in countless fields of endeavor. In music, you'll want to master notes, chords, and scales to play on demand. In the financial world, you'll find fundamentals such as correctly entering data in a double-entry accounting system, creating balance sheets, and preparing income statements. And every sport has some immutable activities or elements that ultimately separate the elite from all the others. In gymnastics you would consider balance a fundamental, and in football, of course, you would include blocking and tackling on your list of fundamentals required for success.

Amazon has mastered the fundamentals of supply chain and distribution. Google is forever pursuing the next level of mastery in search engine technology. Consider the legendary rugby team the New Zealand All Blacks; they attribute a huge part of their dominance to their never-ending pursuit of mastering the fundamentals of their game. In case you are not familiar with this team, they have won 77% of their matches over the last *121 years.*[1, 2] This is the highest winning percentage of any professional sports team over the last century.

In the manufacturing world, Toyota has dedicated itself to mastering the fundamentals of the Toyota Production System, making it a perennial leader in new car quality. Their goal of Six Sigma quality, or 3.4 defects per million attempts, has set them apart.[3] Again, this list could go on and on. The fundamentals in any field, consistently embraced and executed, enable individuals, teams, and organizations to excel!

The world of leadership is no different. If you want to consistently perform at your highest level and make the greatest contribution possible, you need to learn, understand, apply, and pursue mastery of a short list of fundamentals.

UNCOMMON LEADERSHIP

The fundamentals of rugby, manufacturing, accounting, medicine, and most other disciplines are known and well-documented. What about leadership? This is the question Chick-fil-A was asking many years ago. The question was not born of mere curiosity. The organization *needed* to know the answer so that it could accelerate leadership development. Why the need for more leaders? Two primary reasons.

One, you'll never outgrow your leadership. If you don't have enough leaders, you'll stunt your growth, effectiveness, and performance. Also, if your current leaders cannot lead at the next level, you'll never make it there. As John Maxwell has said for years, "Leaders are the lid on any organization."[4]

Next, when you have problems to solve and opportunities to seize, a typical response is to assign a leader. Without an ample supply of "ready-now" leaders, the organization is forced to either miss the opportunities, leave the problems unsolved, or assign them to existing leaders. Don't be deceived. Giving more and more to your existing leaders is a recipe for disaster. The right long-term answer is to grow more leaders.

If you attempt to grow more leaders without a common, behaviorally based definition of leadership, your efforts will be plagued with inefficiency, waste, and frustration.

Twenty-five years ago, Mark was asked by Chick-fil-A to lead a team charged with accelerating leadership development. The group quickly decided their first step was to define the fundamentals of leadership. Only then could the organization begin to strategically and systematically recruit, select, train, develop, and reward those who practiced them. After two years of research and debate, the group assembled in an attempt to distill all they learned into something approachable and applicable to move the organization into the future. The result: the Fundamentals of Uncommon Leadership.

Exactly what do we mean when we say Uncommon Leader? An Uncommon Leader is one who consistently produces elite levels of performance and unleashes the greatness resident within those they lead.

For our purposes here, we'll give you an overview of each of the fundamentals and share tangible and tactical ideas you can begin to apply right away. This is the pattern we'll repeat throughout this book. All you must provide is the will to take the next step. Let's explore the Fundamentals of Uncommon Leadership.

Fundamental #1

SEE THE FUTURE

The ability to determine how you want the future to be different from today.

What's your picture of the future? This is a critical question. Unfortunately, many leaders are fuzzy on their response. This lack of clarity makes it impossible to lead well. People are looking to their leaders to answer one or more of several critical questions:

- Where are we (team, department, or organization) going?
- What are we trying to accomplish?
- What are we working to become?
- Why does it matter?

These can be incredibly challenging questions! Seeing the future is tricky. At the same time, what a privilege! To envision a future that does not yet exist and rally people to make it a reality is one of the most significant roles a leader plays. But beware, the busier you become, the more difficult it will be to stay clear on the vision. And if the vision is fuzzy to you, it will be blurry, at best, to the people who are following you. That's why we've been saying for decades leadership always begins with a picture of the future.

Articulating your preferred future is not an academic exercise. Purpose-driven companies, those with a clear picture of the future, experience higher market share gains and grow on average three times faster than their competitors, all the while achieving higher employee and customer satisfaction.[5]

We want to acknowledge the challenge this fundamental represents. Don't be deterred. The insight you need can only be found in the struggle to discern your preferred future.

You can do this . . . you must do this. See the Future is the first of the fundamentals for a reason. Would-be followers expect their leaders to have vision. We feel the need to reiterate: Leadership always begins with a picture of the future. No picture, no leadership. No one who aspires to lead well would disagree that we need as much clarity as possible about the future we are asking people to pursue, but how do we identify this future?

Paint the Picture

If you haven't discovered this yet, let us be the first to tell you: If you are the leader, people want to know your intentions—your desired destination. Sometimes people will articulate their question and other times they'll just wait to see. But you can rest assured, people always want to know where you are attempting to take the organization. And, more importantly, they want to know why they should help you get there.

Again, leadership always begins with a picture of the future. To create a compelling picture, you will need a new skill: You must be able to see the unseen. People not only expect this of us as leaders; they need us to fulfill this role in several ways.

- **We are expected** to see the changing landscape in our industry—before it changes.
- **We are asked** to see the outcome of potential strategies years before the final verdict can be rendered.
- **We are expected** to see the potential in people before their potential has been translated into performance.
- **We must have** a vision of the future we are attempting to create for our organization.

For some leaders and aspiring leaders, this fundamental is daunting. Whether Seeing the Future energizes you or terrifies you, it will be this ability that allows you to enter the ranks of true leadership. If you've read anything about leadership, you'll know this picture of the future is often referred to as vision. Vision is more than an indispensable ingredient for effective leadership; it is the cornerstone.

As a leader, this is the step in your leadership journey when you synthesize all you know to be true with what you want to be true. When your experience, judgment, creativity, intuition, and knowledge collide to create your picture of a preferred future, that is the moment in which your vision is born.

The process of coalescing all of the above will require time. How much? We don't know. However, the goal is to create a vivid picture of the future. The more vibrant the colors and the more details you can provide, the more likely you are to create a compelling future others will be interested in pursuing with you.

Here are a few questions you need to answer to help you Paint the Picture for all to see. Your responses should reflect your scope of leadership. If you are leading a team, think about your team. If you are an organizational leader, think bigger.

- What do you want to be true in the future that is not true today?
- If you could single-mindedly pursue only one goal for the next decade, what would it be?
- Why is it important for you to accomplish your vision?
- What accomplishment are you willing to invest your life and career on?
- What are you working to become? Why does it matter?
- What are you convinced that your organization should endlessly and tirelessly strive for?
- What is big enough that you could work toward it your entire career and then pass the baton to others to pursue?

Review your answers to these questions. What picture is emerging?

Leaders are the architects of the future. You were born for this! Don't make the common mistake of assuming this is someone else's job. Every leader must have a vision for what they've been entrusted to steward. The difference between the CEO's vision and the frontline leader's is breadth and time horizon, but both still need vision to lead well.

A CEO is often thinking about a decade or more into the future, considering market dynamics, the probable impact of new technologies, the next competitive advantage, and they are placing Strategic Bets on reinvestment that may not see a return for years. A frontline leader in a retail environment needs vision as well. She should be concerned about the experience she is trying to lead her team to create during a given shift, the cost implications of her decisions on this month's Profit and Loss statement, and ways to raise the engagement level of her employees today.

Peter Drucker, the world-renowned leadership guru, famously and accurately said, "The best way to predict the future is to create it."[6] We agree with Dr. Drucker, but you have to see it before you can create it.

> ## ┌ PRACTICE!
>
> Leadership always begins with a picture of the future. What's yours? If your answer is unclear, begin devoting time to answer this crucial question. When you have clarity on your preferred future, in that moment, your leadership journey has officially begun.

*For more ideas on Seeing the Future, download the free PDF "How to Create a Vision That Inspires," **https://leadeveryday.com/vision**, or scan this QR code:*

Fundamental #2

ENGAGE AND DEVELOP OTHERS

To help those you lead care deeply about their work, coworkers, customers, and the organization while also fueling their growth.

Engagement is a prerequisite for sustained excellence over time and one of the primary drivers of discretionary effort and creativity in the workplace. In many ways, engagement has become the shorthand metric to judge the vitality of an organization's culture.

We think this is a bit risky. Engagement is not the goal; performance is the goal. However, lifting and stewarding the engagement of those we lead is a fundamental of Uncommon Leadership. Engagement, channeled appropriately, enables execution, and execution is the linchpin to elite performance. Let's explore one idea to help you engage those who matter most: the men and women whom you must convince to help turn your vision into reality—the people who work in your organization.

Cast the Vision

Assuming you have completed the activity in the previous section (Paint the Picture), you should have emerging clarity on what you are trying to accomplish. Congratulations! Now you have the opportunity to begin sharing your vision with those you ultimately hope to enroll to help make the vision a reality. Communicating the vision will take many forms over time, including your actions and the symbols, systems, and mechanisms you put in place to reinforce the vision. But as is most often the case, we suggest you be the initial messenger of the vision. You must be able to say it before others can see it.

If you are a seasoned leader, the following recommendation will not surprise you. Experience has taught you that one size does not fit all when communicating vision, so we're suggesting you create at least four versions of your message. You don't have to create these in any specific order; however, if you follow the order suggested below, the entire process will be easier. We do believe you'll ultimately need all of the following versions of your vision.

A keynote presentation—Assume for a moment you have the chance to cast your vision to your entire organization or speak at an industry conference; you've been given 40 minutes—a full keynote address. What would you say? What stories would you tell? What visuals would you use to support your presentation? You need to write it down. Prepare as if you will be given this opportunity in the coming weeks. The depth of thinking required to complete this activity will provide much of the content you'll need to complete the balance of this **Practice!** assignment.

A blog post—You'll encounter some situations where you can't say as much as you could in a keynote presentation. Maybe you're on a podcast, or in a meeting with a potential client or potential vendor. Some leaders make appearances in new employee orientation sessions. In all of these settings you can't say as much as you did in the keynote; what would you say? Think in terms of 1,000 words—a good, medium-length blog post. What would you write? This statement could serve as the basis for your remarks in any of the situations mentioned above and many others. Write it down.

An elevator speech—There are times when you want to share your vision more quickly. What would you tell someone if you stepped into an elevator together for a ride to the 25th floor? You have about 90 seconds. What would you say? Write it down. Anytime you need a quick version of your vision, you'll be ready.

A slogan—Finally, there are times when a well-worded phrase or pithy statement will be exactly what you need, not to explain the vision, but to represent it in its most succinct form. This is when a slogan will be perfect. We know there is extreme risk in suggesting this. As leaders, we must never succumb to the temptation to allow our leadership and our vision to fall victim to sloganeering. Slogans devoid of strategy, discipline, and leadership commitment may be clever but they never transform hearts and minds. Strategic alignment and action are the key attributes of a well-conceived slogan. The depth of thinking you've invested in the previous facets of this assignment is the antidote for catchy taglines devoid of real, heartfelt meaning.

If you can create a single, compelling, and preferably catchy phrase that truly represents the essence of your vision, you will be miles ahead of your competition. Think of this as the shorthand version of a dream rich with meaning and significance.

Here are a few examples to spark your imagination:

Apple: Think Different[7]
Disney: Create Magical Experiences[8]
IDEO: Design for a Better World[9]
Google: Organize the World's Information[10]
TED: Ideas Change Everything[11]
Netflix: Entertain the World[12]
Red Bull: Give Wings to People and Ideas[13]
Lead Every Day: Change Your World[14]

Regardless of the language you use to communicate vision, any slogan should be clear and succinct. Peter Drucker said it like this, "The effective mission statement is short and sharply focused. It should fit on a T-shirt."[15]

What are you going to put on your T-shirt?

PRACTICE!

Schedule time to complete the assignment outlined above. Given the scope and time required, we recommend breaking up the activity into at least four time blocks over the next 30 days.

Fundamental #3
REINVENT CONTINUOUSLY

The never-ending pursuit of improved skills, methods, and outcomes.

We frequently talk to leaders who struggle with this fundamental. Few leaders have been taught the skill set or the mindset necessary to reinvent well. Add to this the fact that few leaders are modeling these behaviors and it is no surprise a gap exists in this arena.

Leaders must be careful—there is a gravitational pull toward what is known. Unfortunately, the best answer is rarely the status quo. Leaders who cannot reinvent are destined for irrelevance, or worse. In our dynamic world, leaders who can't Reinvent Continuously are likely to be looking for another job—or, more likely, another profession. Consider the S&P 500. Since its conception in 1955, only 52 of the original 500 companies are still on the list![16]

Progress is always preceded by change. Too many leaders look at change as a burden, an obstacle, an inconvenience, and in extreme cases, something to be avoided at all costs. On the contrary, orchestrating and leading positive, sustained change in service of the vision is our job! Leaders who don't lead change could be legitimately challenged as to whether they are even leading at all.

Let's suppose you want to strengthen your ability to Reinvent Continuously. What can you do?

Retrain Your Brain
Here's a really quick neuroscience lesson: The brain is a self-optimizing memory system. When faced with a problem, challenge, or opportunity, our natural tendency is to default to what is known. This is a helpful feature of our brain when faced with a survival situation. However, when working in the creative realm,

it's somewhat of a bug we must work to overcome. The known is always at odds with the new. So, what do you do? You learn how the brain works and create new neural pathways that allow you to explore what is possible.

One approach to overcome our brain's natural tendency to follow well-worn mental ruts is to learn any number of techniques to help us divert our thinking on command. We can redirect our thoughts to places we've never been before, just as we might change the direction of water flowing down a hillside. We call this brain training.

There are hundreds of techniques to help us move beyond what is known. Some of the better-known methods include Consider the Opposite, Random Input, Jamming, Brain Writing, Quotas, and Mind Mapping. The most frequently attempted of these techniques is Brainstorming.

The next time you are facing a challenging problem or an apparent opportunity, suggest the group conduct a brainstorming session. Now, for many of you, this is the absolute last thing you want to do. We understand. The vast majority—think 90%—of the brainstorming sessions you've been in across your career have been *useless*. That's not the fault of the tool. If a person cannot use a chef's knife effectively, it has nothing to do with the knife. Here are some things you can do to make your next brainstorming session brilliant.

Appoint a facilitator. A prepared and competent facilitator in brainstorming sessions will be the single greatest factor in the success of your efforts—at least in the beginning. Over time, you will want everyone in the group to be well-versed in the role of facilitator, enabling the entire group to work together to ensure the best possible outcomes.

Pinpoint the issue or problem. This may feel like a blinding flash of the obvious, but it can be harder than you think. We have been in far too many brainstorming sessions where the problem statement was broad, squishy, ill-defined, or some combination of the above. Be forewarned: The presenting problem is rarely the real problem; you'll have to dig deeper to find the root cause of the issue.

Visually display all ideas. This is one of the most critical elements for great brainstorming sessions. If we could, we would buy every organization in the world a flip chart—or two! When you display the proceedings, there are two primary benefits. First, the person sharing an idea knows it has been captured satisfactorily and can release it mentally. Secondly, when the participants can see all the ideas visually displayed, there is a good chance new ideas will be sparked in the process. Don't be surprised if you hear something like this: "Let's combine idea #17 with #128—that would create something new." We know this recommendation is more difficult in a virtual world. However, there are a number of tools and techniques you can employ to allow virtual participants to see the ideas being shared.

Go for quantity, not quality. This may feel strange to many of you. Why wouldn't we want *quality* ideas? Certainly, you do want amazing ideas to surface. However, brainstorming is much like mining for gold or precious gems. The process demands you move tons of dirt (aka bad ideas) to find your prize.

Invest sufficient time. Brainstorming typically occurs on two levels. In level one, you document what is already known. Most often, there are few insights or breakthroughs in level one. Level two is the domain of the new, innovative, and previously unknown. On average, the time investment required to enter level two is 45 minutes. If you've ever been in a failed brainstorming session, chances are good you didn't invest enough time.

Doug Hall operates an innovation think tank. He and his team help organizations solve their biggest challenges. His team has worked with over 2,000 organizations and has created and tested over 26,000 innovations for 3M, American Express, AT&T, Apple, Mercedes-Benz, and so many more. If you hire Doug, his first brainstorming session will last 16 hours and be spread over two days.[17]

We're not suggesting all your brainstorming sessions should last two days. But don't miss the point: Brainstorming as a technique to unearth innovative ideas requires a significant investment of time and energy.

PRACTICE!

Look for an opportunity to try the ideas above in the next 30 days. Pull out your calendar and, if possible, schedule it now. Even if you are not the team leader, you can volunteer to facilitate an upcoming brainstorming session.

For a more expansive and detailed list of ideas, check out our free PDF on Brilliant Brainstorming at **https://leadeveryday.com/brainstorming-tips**, *or scan this QR code:*

Fundamental #4

VALUE RESULTS AND RELATIONSHIPS

To ensure sustained levels of elite performance while honoring those we lead.

What's the most challenging part of leadership for you personally? We're going to guess this fundamental might be your greatest struggle, and here's why: After sharing this content around the world for decades, our experience tells us most leaders have a natural bias. There is either a compass in our head or a magnet in our heart that guides our actions. We are either results-oriented or relationship-oriented. We didn't ask to see the world this way; we just do. Without conscious effort, our bias will rule our actions. While this is natural and understandable, this is not the path of Uncommon Leaders. If we want to maximize performance, we must learn to value *both.*

By the way, we've encountered a ridiculously small percentage of extraordinary leaders who naturally value both. For them, leadership is just easier. If this is you, you can skip ahead. For about 99% of you, please keep reading. Yes, 99%! Randy has asked thousands of leaders in his events: "*Which way does your boss lean—results or relationships?*" Less than 1% said both. Almost every leader has a bias.

Compensate for Your Bias

Before you can compensate for your bias, you must acknowledge your bias. Don't deny, hide, deflect, or apologize for it—own it. Both of us have a results bias. We have been working to compensate and place more value on relationships for decades. Fortunately, we have some outstanding team members who are more relationship-oriented to help us. Once you own your bias, you can begin to mitigate its impact on your leadership. As you read the ideas below, remember the goal is not to change your hardwiring; your bias will always exist. However, the best leaders always strive to value *both* results and relationships.

The process required to value both results and relationships is simple, much like getting a pair of prescription eyeglasses. The critical step is determining what level of correction you need. Are you extremely farsighted or just marginally? The answer matters. Armed with the knowledge of your bias, all you need to do is determine what people, mechanisms, or systems you need to put in place to help you elevate what you don't do naturally well. Here are a few examples to stimulate your thinking:

- Add someone to your leadership team or inner circle of advisors who has a different bias than yours (e.g., if you are more results-oriented, be sure you have someone close to you who is more relationship-oriented).
- If you are more results-oriented, try setting a goal for the number of notes of encouragement, gratitude, and appreciation you'll write over the next year, and track your progress.
- If you're more relationship-oriented, set some performance goals for yourself and help your team do the same. Share the goals, monitor your progress, and take corrective action if you're not on track. If you do hit your milestones, celebrate!

PRACTICE!

Decide what you'll do initially to compensate for your bias and give it a try. You may need more or less correction to value *both* results and relationships. Continue to experiment until you have it dialed in.

Fundamental #5

EMBODY A LEADER'S HEART

To live and lead in a fashion that makes you a leader people want to follow.

More than 25 years ago, Mark and his team began their official quest to help Chick-fil-A systematically accelerate leadership development. The fundamentals we are exploring together were one of the outcomes of their journey. The original team also determined that a picture of leadership might be helpful. They selected an iceberg.

We believe this is a perfect metaphor for leadership. As you may recall from your elementary days, about 10% of an iceberg is above the waterline. In most cases, you can easily discern a person's leadership skills and competency by merely observing them. The first four fundamentals are all above the waterline. However, the vast majority of a leader's impact will be determined by what lies below the waterline—the 90% below the surface. This is the domain of the heart.

Our fifth fundamental, Embody a Leader's Heart, will ultimately determine the level of impact and opportunity we have as leaders.

If your heart is not right, no one cares about your skills.

HEART WORK

As leaders, we should always be working on our heart. What does that look like? We've identified five heart habits we need to continually cultivate in our life and leadership. The result: a new heart and the gradual transformation into a leader people want to follow. We'll provide a quick overview of the first four habits and then take a deeper dive into the final one.

Hunger for Wisdom. *Continuously seek knowledge and experiences to fuel improved judgment and discernment allowing for improved decision-making.*

A hunger for wisdom is a condition of the heart and is born of the humility needed to lead well and fueled by the desire to learn and grow. This humble posture reveals a teachable spirit. The arrogant are not the best learners or leaders.

Expect the Best. *Adopt an optimistic spirit born of a genuine belief in yourself and those around you to impact the future.*

The best leaders are certainly grounded in reality. However, they don't let their current realities steal their dreams. Good leaders have a high internal locus of control—a term from psychology that roughly translates to an individual's belief in their ability to affect future outcomes. If you do not believe you can rally others to create a preferred future, why are you attempting to lead?

Accept Responsibility. *Willingly accept the outcomes and missed opportunities under your authority regardless of your actual direct involvement.*

The men and women who embrace this heart habit of accepting responsibility are quick to do so when things don't work out. They embrace the idea that they are responsible not only for their own actions, but the actions and outcomes of those they lead. The exception is when their team excels—the Uncommon Leader always allows others to shine and shares credit for the work.

Respond with Courage. *Lead based on conviction and character in the face of uncertainty.*

Virtually everything you do as a leader requires courage. Sometimes in small doses and other times in massive amounts. Examples of when you need courage include choosing whom to assign to a crucial project, deciding when a reorganization is needed, determining which strategies will best position your organization for the future, selecting which products and services to discontinue, or giving hard feedback to a trusted employee. The list is endless. The good news: Courage is like a muscle—the more you use it, the stronger it will become.

Think Others First. *Escape the gravitational pull of self-serving behaviors and focus your energy on releasing the untapped potential of those you serve.*

If an Uncommon Leader had a single defining characteristic, this would be it. Yes, all the fundamentals and heart habits matter, but this one is different. The ability to Think Others First is the ultimate reflection of a leader's heart.

As we reflect on our past, our best days and our shining moments always occurred when we were focused on others. This can be your reality as well.

Here's an activity to help you Think Others First as your default—a lifestyle rather than an occasional response.

The process begins with a conscious effort to shift our focus from ourselves to others. What many leaders find helpful is a cue or trigger to short-circuit the gravity-generating mechanism resident in our own heart and mind that pulls us to think about ourselves more than others. You may be thinking, *Okay, a trigger . . . Do you have any to recommend? How do you shift your focus?* We're glad you asked!

We want to challenge you to try an experiment:

Try to add value to every person you meet over the next 24 hours.

We've shared this idea enough over the years to know what most of you are thinking. *What you're asking me to do is impossible. There's no way I can add value to every person I encounter over the next 24 hours.* Hold on. You didn't read the assignment carefully enough. Go back and read it again.

Do you see anything you missed the first time? Right, the word *try* is pivotal in this assignment. Here's why.

If you are *trying* to add value to another human being, who are you thinking about? Them, of course. Remember, this activity is to help you shift your focus from yourself to others. The impact this activity will have on your life and leadership does not hinge on your success rate or your batting average. This would be impossible to measure anyway. The transformation you seek is in the *trying*.

How do you add value to others? This is another fantastic

question! We would love for you to make your own list, but we'll give you a few ideas to jump-start your thinking.

- Encourage them.
- Recognize them.
- Coach them.
- Show empathy.
- Ask their opinion.
- Offer a genuine compliment.
- Thank them.
- If you're a person of faith, offer a silent prayer.
- Be present during hard times.
- Provide resources (e.g., a podcast or book recommendation).

PRACTICE!

On several of the previous **Practice!** activities, we've asked you to look at your calendar or find an opportunity over the coming weeks—this one is different. We want you to look at your watch right now. What time is it? For the next 24 hours, try to add value to every person you meet. If you choose to persist with this effort beyond this initial experiment, over time, your heart and your leadership will change.

In 1973, a horse named Secretariat made history. At the time, he was only the ninth horse to win the Triple Crown—the Kentucky Derby, the Preakness, and the Belmont Stakes. He didn't just win these races; he set records in each race that still stand today, over 50 years later. He set a pace in the Belmont that allowed him to win that race by 31 lengths. That's over 80 yards! Some believe that race was the greatest ever run by a thoroughbred.[18]

In October 1989, Secretariat contracted laminitis, a fatal hoof condition, and had to be euthanized. During the necropsy, Dr. Thomas Swerczek, a veterinary pathologist from the University of Kentucky, made a remarkable discovery. Secretariat's heart was estimated to weigh 22 pounds! The typical thoroughbred's heart weighs in at only eight and a half pounds. This explains the power and endurance of the mighty horse. His heart multiplied his skills. But make no mistake, the power Secretariat demonstrated was not about heart alone. If you had put the same oversized heart in a mule, it would not have won the Triple Crown. Secretariat had talent, for sure, but his heart made all the difference.[19]

The same is true for leaders. You really can become a leader people want to follow. If we can Embody a Leader's Heart and learn to Think Others First, it will multiply our skills and transform us into an exceptionally rare Uncommon Leader.

Now you know the fundamentals of Uncommon Leaders—and you know their secret. If you want to Become a Better Leader, you must SERVE.

See the Future
Engage and Develop Others
Reinvent Continuously
Value Results and Relationships
Embody a Leader's Heart

What we are advocating here is the highest form of leadership, yet it remains misunderstood and undervalued. The fact that these fundamentals are countercultural should not discourage you from pursuing them. They will set you and your performance apart in a world of mediocrity. We encourage you to always SERVE.

For a deeper dive beyond what we covered in this chapter, you may want to read Mark's book Uncommon Greatness.

CREATE CLARITY

If you can't explain it simply, you don't understand it well enough.
—**Albert Einstein**

What was the best gift you ever received as a child? As an adult? In many cases, our greatest gifts were those we could not give ourselves. Perhaps they were too costly, or they were one-of-a-kind creations, or maybe they were something we never anticipated. That new bike or handmade card from a child may no longer bring the joy it once did, but for a moment or a season, it was life-giving.

Now, consider a gift you can provide the people on your team, one that will bring greater levels of joy, purpose, fulfillment, and success to every one of them. Oh, and by the way, it's something they cannot give themselves. What is it? The answer is clarity. Beyond leadership, nothing has greater impact on people and performance than clarity, and leaders are the only ones who can give it.

For context regarding why clarity in the workplace matters so much, we need to acknowledge the fact that the men and women on your team will likely invest 100,000 hours of their lives at work. We know. The first time we heard this number, we were overwhelmed with disbelief. Do the math. With some generally accepted assumptions, the length of a typical career, and some modestly conservative projections regarding hours worked per week (plus your commute), you have a whopping number that for many exceeds 100,000 hours.[1]

Years ago, Mark had an experience that underscores the importance of this chapter on clarity. Having just assumed a new role and the responsibility for an existing department within his organization, his first meeting with the new team was eye-opening.

After being introduced by the president of the company, Mark offered the anticipated greetings and excitement for the opportunity to partner with this group of talented professionals. Only a few moments into his impromptu remarks, a young woman raised her hand.

"Yes, do you have a question?"

"What's the vision?" she asked.

Before we continue the story, let us ask you a question: Does the woman's question surprise you? It shouldn't. People expect their leaders to have vision, whether you've been their leader for five years or, in Mark's case, five minutes.

In response to the question, Mark began to describe a future in which the people assembled would have more reach, impact, and influence in the organization. Before he could elaborate, the woman stopped him.

"I'm not talking about any of that," she responded.

"What is it you want to know?"

"I want to know if my programs are going to continue. Where will I sit? And, who will be my supervisor?"

"I don't know the answer to any of your questions," Mark said. "But what I do know is that we are going to have more reach, impact, and influence in the years to come. We'll work together in the weeks and months ahead to answer your specific questions."

For years, Mark lacked the language to describe that day's events until he heard Andy Stanley say, "People want certainty but will settle for clarity."[2] This woman wanted certainty. Her questions, if answered in the terms she wanted, would require specific answers well beyond what a new leader would know. All Mark had to offer was clarity—he could speak with confidence about his strategic intent. This form of clarity is one of the greatest gifts we can ever provide to the people we serve.

Now, a final word on this woman's situation. She was expressing more than questions. She was revealing her mindset and most likely her anxiety about a future where she feared she would have no control and perhaps no input. As leaders, we must be careful not to overlook or dismiss the legitimate angst of those we lead. Clarity did not resolve this woman's uncertainty. However, in the moment, it was all that was available. Over the weeks and months that followed, all her questions, stated and unstated, were addressed.

In this example, the woman had a legitimate question regarding the vision. Make no mistake, this is something people want to know. Therefore, you need to make it as clear as possible. However, we'll say no more about vision here. If you'd like a review on crafting a compelling vision, you can go back to the previous chapter (pages 29–52).

In the balance of this chapter, we'll talk about several other opportunities for you to provide the gift of clarity. When you do, you will eliminate much of the confusion, frustration, hesitation, and, in extreme cases, chaos that plagues the modern workplace. You will discover the liberating power of clarity.

CHAMPION CLARITY

Randy used to wear corrective lenses for waning eyesight, and then the most amazing thing happened—LASIK surgery. In five minutes, everything changed. The first night after the procedure, he remembers awakening and opening his eyes at 2:11 AM and seeing the numbers on the alarm clock were crystal, high-def clear. It was life-changing! We wish we could zap the people you lead with five minutes of leadership LASIK and they would have lasting clarity, but we can't. Creating clarity is your never-ending job.

For the remainder of this chapter, we're going to assume that you are the newly appointed Champion of Clarity. Your superpower is to provide others with the gift of clarity. Following are several opportunities for you to use your power for good.

Clarify Roles

For decades, we have participated in organizational health assessments in one form or another. We've even created our own. Mark created his first in 1983. It was really more about the team's assessment of his performance as their leader, but it was a precursor to the more modern assessments many organizations use today. One issue that consistently surfaces in many of these assessments is a lack of role clarity. Of all the challenges organizations face, this one is clearly on us as leaders.

This is such a big deal. When dealing with individuals, we recommend that role setting should always precede goal setting. Do you and your individual team members know their roles? Our guess is they assume they do, but would you agree with their conclusions?

Role setting is not about the person's title. What are the key things the organization expects from the person? You can represent these as an archetype or as the activities you want people to engage in. Over the years, our roles have included scout, architect, coach, trainer, teacher, consultant, ambassador, and more. When using the specific activities approach, we've both been charged with the responsibility to curate, collaborate, and create. Regardless of which approach you take, every role should be accompanied by a simple description of no more than a few sentences.

For next-level impact, you can assign a target time allocation to each role. Then, when planning the allocation of your time, you can program to your targets. As an example, if your target is to invest 20% of your time creating, you could block one day a week (at least in concept). Mark would say the most strategic and productive years of his career were the result of this approach. To make this even *more* powerful, track your time against your targets. This will provide more accountability and urgency to strategically steward your time.

How confident are you that everyone in your organization has role clarity? You can help them.

┌─ PRACTICE! ─

Identify *your* four to six key roles. Then, ask everyone on your team to do the same. As mentioned, the next level of impact beyond clarifying roles is investing your time strategically. Talk with your leader about how he or she wants you to steward your time.

Clarify the Win

Most people love to win. Even those who wouldn't describe themselves as competitive, if they are honest, don't like to lose. Every leader can give the gift of clarity by defining the win. What does success look like? How will we know if we win? Are there any metrics we can rely on to define our level of success? The answer to all these questions should be yes.

At an event, we asked the attendees to text members of their team and ask them to name the top three priorities for their business in the coming year (a slight variation on the question "what constitutes a win?"). Later that evening, a leader shared that all three of the folks she texted had the same answer, even using the same language. Randy said, "Congratulations!" The leader said, "No, those aren't our top priorities! We are perfectly aligned ... on the wrong things." Without reading too much into this scenario, it would appear as though this leader had not provided the gift of clarity regarding what a win looks like. The good news: She owned it by telling Randy, "Their lack of clarity is on me."

If you're feeling bold, text several members of your team and ask them a similar question: "What are our top three goals this year?" Or, "What constitutes a 'win' this year?" Or, "What are our top three priorities this year?" Or, however you want to ask the question. You are testing your alignment on what matters most. The responses you receive are a direct reflection of the clarity you have provided.

Sometimes the win can be represented as a clearly articulated goal. If you do set goals, you'll get more bang for your efforts if you write them down.

Dr. Gail Matthews, a psychology professor at the Dominican University of California, validated the power of written goals. Her study found that individuals who wrote down their goals were significantly more likely to achieve them than those who did not. In fact, it increased their chances by a whopping 42%![3]

A recent example from the world of Chick-fil-A (CFA) fits here. As mentioned earlier, each location is independently operated. However, corporate decides where the locations will be placed and who will operate them. A few years ago, one of Chick-fil-A's local Operators hired our team at Lead Every Day to help him map out the next steps for his business. The Operator decided he wanted to earn the opportunity to operate a second CFA location. This quest is referred to as the Multi-Restaurant Opportunity (MRO) selection process. This is no trivial pursuit. If a second restaurant is awarded, it will typically translate to millions of dollars in personal income for the Operator over the next decade.

With the goal clearly identified, our team began helping the local team implement the Lead Every Day OS. Their first focus area was to Improve Team Performance. Next, they decided to go all in and Strengthen Their Organization.

The clarity around the win at every step in their process, combined with enough time to prepare, were the keys that allowed this team to be rewarded with an additional restaurant opportunity. We have walked with dozens of leaders on this journey. In every case, the clarity regarding the win invigorates the entire team.

```
┌─ PRACTICE! ────────────────────────────────┐
│                                             │
│  What does a win look like for you? What personal and     │
│  professional goals are you pursuing? What three to five  │
│  goals would help your team or organization find some     │
│  much-needed clarity? Have you clearly defined a win for  │
│  those in your organization? If not, begin the process of │
│  defining the win right away.                             │
│                                             │
└─────────────────────────────────────────────┘
```

Clarify the Charter

We have been asked, "What is the most important factor in the success of a new team?" Your mind may go to the leadership, team membership, the budget, the time horizon, or something else. If we're talking about a functional or operating team, we can make a persuasive case for the team leader. However, if we're talking about a project team, our answer is the Team Charter.

We are not fans of templates. The truth is the world is dynamic and context matters, and templates often miss the context. For leaders, we prefer to provide elements, factors to consider, or guidelines to stimulate your thinking. No two charters we've ever created followed the same outline. A charter, like most of the things in this book, is a tool, not a law. Modify the list below as you see fit and use it to help your teams be more successful. Don't miss the point—the more you clarify the assignment, the greater your odds of success.

Team Charter: Key Elements

Purpose—Why does this team exist? To solve a problem? To make a recommendation? To create a product? To reinvent a process? There should be no mystery regarding the purpose of the team.

Deliverables—Deliverables provide the specifics that are often not included in a purpose statement. For example, if a team's purpose is to make a recommendation on regional offices, the deliverables might include a timeline, staffing plan, budget, return on investment projections, and success metrics.

Key Milestones—When is the work to be completed? Are there target dates that need to be met (e.g., first draft, prototype)? Are there approvals needed along the way? If so, when and by whom?

Design Principles—Any decisions that have already been made prior to the work of the team beginning that directly affect their work process or deliverables should be stated as design principles. Are there any predetermined expectations that must be incorporated into the final output? If so, include them in the charter. Here are a few examples: All prototypes will be tested in the field for six months before full deployment. Accelerated learning techniques will be incorporated into all classroom sessions. All training sessions will be delivered by senior leaders from our organization.

Boundaries—These can be as unique and diverse as you can imagine. What are the lines that cannot be crossed? For example, if you're designing a training event, a boundary might be that participation is voluntary, or attendees will pay for the training, or no training can take place in the fourth quarter of the year.

Budget—How much money has been allocated to this project? Is this the annual budget or the *total* budget? This will matter if the project will be executed over more than one calendar year. Does the budget cover design and delivery or just design?

Team Membership—Who is on the team? If the members have assigned roles, this is a good place to note that as well. It's also helpful to designate the team leader or facilitator.

Sponsor—Which senior leader has sanctioned the work of this team? We have seen multiple names here. We prefer one name. Who has the team's back and has approved this charter?

A final word of encouragement here: Never lose sight of the goal driving this activity. Team Charters have the potential to create new levels of clarity and performance beyond your expectations.

┌─ PRACTICE!

Create a charter for every new team you form for the rest of your career. If you want to accelerate the success of an existing team, go back and create a charter for them. You could even decide to co-create the charters with the teams.

If you want to download a free worksheet to help you create your Team Charter, go to: **https://leadeveryday.com/charter**, *or scan this QR code:*

Clarify Priorities

We love planning. We believe planning is one of your most significant contributions to your organization. Before you dismiss this as a bias toward bureaucracy, let us explain.

Let's assume you have recruited and selected an amazing group of talented, conscientious, and motivated individuals. Congratulations! If this is true, your challenge is not sloppy work, missed deadlines, or trying to get people to show up for work. The people you have selected will do magnificent work.

Here's the challenge:

You receive no credit for doing the wrong work with excellence.

No level of excellence can overcome the waste of putting your hand to the wrong task. Planning is the process of determining the *right* work. This is why leaders should fully engage in this effort. As we plan, we are directing the time, talent, energy, and financial resources of our organization toward the desired objectives. If we don't do this, who will?

Here's the truth about planning—most of the time, leaders, and anyone else involved in planning, don't know the *right* answer. Charting a course to a future that does not yet exist is as much art as science. Data on the past can help, but intuition, judgment, and courage will be needed in abundance. Planning is at best a calculated bet.

In virtually every scenario, multiple right answers may surface and the success of each option hinges on variables outside a leader's control. When faced with the scenarios, it's important to understand that planning is at best an exercise in corporate gambling. You are placing a bet on the goals, strategies, and tactics you've devised. You're also placing a bet on your people to run the play well.

From time to time during this process of placing your bets, you will discern the need for a disproportionate investment in one area or another. We call this a Strategic Bet. Examples include doubling your investment in technology for a season to close a critical gap or as an attempt to leapfrog your chief competitor, increasing a department or a team's staffing to enable the accomplishment of a special project, or making a significant investment to accelerate leadership development while creating the internal capabilities to sustain your leadership engine indefinitely.

To do any of these, you will most likely have to cut the budget, the staff, or both from another area to pay for this effort. As we practice the concept, a Strategic Bet is not a permanent shift in resource allocation; it's for just a season—maybe one year, perhaps three. You can decide what is required.

We've made Strategic Bets many times over the years and we're guessing you have also, even if you didn't call them by this name. One example from Mark's time at Chick-fil-A seems relevant. During a season when he was leading Training and Development, the question of how the organization should approach staff development came up (and it wasn't the first time). Because the team was responsible for both leadership development and the professional development of individual contributors, there was a continuing debate about how the department's finite budget should be allocated. The decision was made to overinvest, from a percentage perspective, in the leaders, and after the gap in this area was closed, resources would be shifted back toward the balance of the staff. In retrospect, Mark wishes he had made this bet earlier in his tenure.

Now, assuming you see the merits of this argument, what area(s) of your organization could benefit from a focused, disproportionate investment of people or financial resources for a season? Place your bet.

PRACTICE!

Ask your team members individually to articulate your team/organization's priorities. Compare their answers. If you are not aligned, give the gift of clarity and get everyone on the same page. We believe you'll be surprised by the impact of this simple activity.

Clarify Next Steps

Mark was invited to serve on the senior leadership team of a large nonprofit organization as a volunteer. At his first meeting, someone said something that sounded like an Action Item. As a reflexive response, he jumped up and wrote the item on a flip chart along with the senior leader's name. It was obvious the item mentioned would be the senior leader's to complete. Mark then turned to the leader and asked, "When can you get this done?"

The room burst into laughter. Mark's response: "Excuse me, is it not your custom to document your Action Items?" To this, the senior leader said, "No. No, it's not our custom, but I think it's a great idea. I'll have the item completed by Thursday."

Exchanges like this can be defining moments for teams and organizations. Another leader who embraced this idea of documenting Action Items told us it had revolutionized his entire organization. He said their cultural norm for decades had been to talk about things but never do them. Everything changed when they began answering the question: *Who will do what by when?*

Does your team talk about more than they actually do? Someone needs to ask the question, "Is that an Action Item?" If the answer is yes, grab a flip chart and create three columns: the action to be taken, the name of the person who will do it, and the date by which the item will be completed.

By the way, the flip chart step is important. We've been in meetings when an Action Item surfaces and someone says, "I'll take that," and the meeting continues. This is bad form. First, you don't know how the person accepting the action has defined it. You don't know when they will have the item completed. Finally, there is no record to enable group follow-up. When you visually display the item, everyone can agree on its specifics. A completion date is required, and follow-up is ensured because the team will routinely review Action Items for completion.

If you are participating in a virtual meeting, the same principle applies—visually displaying Action Items is significantly better than having one individual keeping notes. For many, communicating effectively in a virtual world is more difficult. Therefore, this practice is even more critical. There are several methods you can use to display your Action Items in an online meeting including a virtual whiteboard, utilizing the chat function, and numerous collaboration tools.

┌─ PRACTICE! ─────────────────────────

During your next meeting, and every meeting, listen for Action Items, then be sure everyone is clear regarding *Who will do what by when.* This is the type of clarity that produces short- and long-term results.

─────────────────────────────────────

DID YOU MEAN FEET OR METERS?

In December 1998, NASA launched the Mars Climate Orbiter. The spacecraft had the dual mission of studying the atmosphere and climate of the Red Planet and serving as a vital communications platform for future voyages to Mars.[4]

On September 23, 1999, the spacecraft disappeared. NASA was able to discern that the orbiter had entered the Martian atmosphere at the wrong angle and was obliterated by the combination of speed, heat, and pressure.[5]

After a complete after-action review, the root cause of the disaster became obvious: Two of the teams working on the orbital insertion calculations had reached different conclusions regarding the angle of entry. Why? One used the imperial unit of pound-force, and the other used the metric unit of newtons. As it turns out, newtons and pound-force are not equivalent.

This lack of clarity cost NASA and the US taxpayers $125 million, a failed mission, and some embarrassing headlines, not to mention delays in the Mars exploration plans.

What is lack of clarity costing your organization?

IMPROVE YOUR EFFECTIVENESS

Efficiency is doing things right; effectiveness is doing the right things.
—Peter Drucker

I f you've read other books we've published, you are probably not surprised we began this chapter with a quote from Peter Drucker. We have many heroes and role models who have informed our leadership over the years. However, Drucker is near the top of the list.

In his groundbreaking 1966 book *The Effective Executive*, Drucker made a case that still reverberates through the hearts, minds, and aspirations of the world's best leaders: "Effectiveness can be learned—and it also has to be learned."[1] Was Drucker right? We say yes, beyond any doubt.

Far too many leaders have confused activity with accomplishment. They have been deceived by the perception of progress when, in reality, they are printing counterfeit bills—the energy they are expending is of no value. Busyness is not the goal.

Why has this misconception of busyness become so prevalent? One reason is that leaders are so encumbered by their current reality that they cannot comprehend a different path, much less the lofty ideal of elite performance sustained over time. Imagine trying to convince a caterpillar it will one day fly—preposterous!

However, what the caterpillar doesn't realize is that it was born to fly . . . so were you. On the following pages, we'll show you how.

ESCAPE THE QUICKSAND

Almost all the leaders we know want to be more effective. They may use different language—perhaps they desire greater impact, better results, a deeper sense of job satisfaction, or public recognition. So, if virtually every leader wants more of something, what's holding them back? The chances are really high that the primary deterrent to improved effectiveness is their current reality.

While conducting research for the book *Smart Leadership*, we discovered an epidemic of leaders who admitted they were unable to do their best work. They knew how to lead but circumstances were preventing them from doing what they knew was required. The immediate follow-up question was, "What are these circumstances impeding your effectiveness?" The answers we received were certainly diverse. They included:

- Busyness
- Distractions
- Complexity
- Resource scarcity
- Turnover

- Meetings
- Email
- Text messages
- Staff shortages
- Lack of training

- Skill gaps
- Fear
- Fatigue
- Success

What do all of these things have in common? Not much, except they are all impediments to a leader's effectiveness. Our team decided three things:

- The list above is certainly incomplete and highly personal.

- The circumstances that impede a leader's effectiveness can change over time.
- Often, these elements will combine to create an even more toxic mix. We decided to name this quagmire "quicksand."

With the full realization that we could not eliminate the quicksand, how could we best serve leaders? Our response: help them escape the mess they find themselves in and equip them with strategies and tactics to stay out.

Yes, but how? There's that question again. We've been asking it for decades and it continues to serve us well. In this case, we determined a leader's skills are insufficient to orchestrate their escape from the quicksand. Yes, skills matter, but a leader who knows how to swim will still have trouble doing so mired in the mess we just described. The path to escape is paved with our choices.

We identified four Smart Choices to help you escape the quicksand and improve your effectiveness.

In this chapter, we'll review each choice and share a few best practices to help answer our ever-present question: Yes, but how?

Choice #1

CONFRONT REALITY

Confront Reality to stay grounded in truth and lead from a position of strength.

Do you know a leader who is unwilling or unable to Confront Reality? Have you been that leader? From time to time, we all have. The list of reasons for failure in this area are many—sometimes it's simply a blind spot; other times our optimism overrides reality, and, if we're honest, from time to time, we really don't want to know the truth. However, if we are not grounded in the truth, we will never lead from a position of strength.

One famous example of this truth that worked out well for the world was during World War II. As the Germans were attempting to subjugate much of Europe, Hitler's war room was in a panic. If the German army was not doing well on a particular front and the news was reported to the führer, he was outraged. Reportedly, as his tantrums became more extreme and his trust in his generals began to erode, the men providing the information, fearing his reactions, began falsifying the reports.[2]

Crazy, right? Yes, of course.

Certainly, this behavior was an outlier . . . maybe. Do you think people around you are 100% transparent with you? Do you believe they share all the news with you? Let's assume you are not going to become violent. However, who wants to tell the boss her idea is not working? Who on your team might be fearful to share the latest employee engagement data with you? Maybe the facilitator puts the market share report that reflects your lagging performance at the bottom of the agenda in hopes you'll run out of time before the information is shared. Does your administrative assistant warn people before they enter your office about your current mood? All of these things happen in the modern organization. Some of them happen in your world.

It is impossible for you to lead well if you don't know the facts. This first choice is real—will you ignore, explain, deflect, or Confront Reality? But we're getting ahead of ourselves. Before you can *confront* reality, you must know the truth.

Find Fresh Eyes

How do you stay connected to reality in your world? How's that working out for you? How confident are you that you know the truth? You may be wondering, "How do I know the truth about what?" Uncommon Leaders want to know the truth about all areas of their life: their relationships, health and fitness, personal finances, their leadership, team, organization, effectiveness of key strategies, competitive landscape, and more.

While there are many strategies and tactics to help you activate this first choice, one of the most powerful and widely applicable is the idea of Fresh Eyes. This involves actively and proactively seeking outside perspective. This could be a family member, a friend, or any of the individuals mentioned below. The critical point is to avoid attempting to see everything for yourself. You have blind spots. Simply stated, others can see what you cannot. Therefore, in order to combat this reality, you need others to share their unique perspective. You must seek them out. Here are several ways you can do this.

Hire a Coach—Have you ever thought about why the best athletes have a coach? Is a coach really necessary? What value do they add? There is a direct correlation between elite levels of performance and the presence of a coach. You see this same pattern well beyond the world of sports—the best chess players, musicians, writers, and more, often have coaches. In the business world, having a coach can have an outsized return. One study showed 39% of CEOs have an outside coach and 60% of growth-stage CEOs have a coach.[3]

A good coach will provide:

- Perspective
- Insight
- Great questions
- Confidence

- Accountability
- A sounding board
- Documented next steps
- Return on investment

What does all of this yield for the leader? According to the International Coaching Federation, executive coaching yields

70% improvement in individual performance, 50% for the team, and 48% improvement in organizational performance.[4]

If you're looking for Fresh Eyes, the right coach can supercharge your personal effectiveness and your performance.

For a free PDF on "10 Questions to Ask a Potential Coach," go to **https://leadeveryday.com/coaching-questions,** *or scan this QR code:*

Find a Mentor—Have you ever had a mentor? We are blessed to have had many over the years. Many of you may be wondering, "How is a mentor different from a coach?" Great question! Although there are probably some technical differences, an uncomplicated way to think about it is that what coaches do for a fee, mentors do for free. Now, we'll be quick to add, the best coaches play at a level few mentors can. The best coaches are well-practiced in serving their clients. Many mentors have little or no experience in the role. Even fewer have the type of training many coaches have been subjected to. However, don't hear us knocking a good mentor. We've had some extremely helpful ones over the years.

Here are a few tips if you want to leverage what a mentor can offer:

- **Narrow your topic.** Don't expect a single mentor to be able to help you with relationships, finances, communications, and strategy. If you need support in all of these areas, you probably need multiple mentors.
- **Drive the agenda.** Let your mentor know what topic or

topics you would like guidance on. A best practice is to send a few questions to your mentor 48 hours in advance of your conversation. This is not for your mentor—this preparation is for you.

- **Listen more than you talk.** Follow-up questions will be your most powerful tool to extract maximum value from your time together.

Hire a Consultant—Often, you'll find yourself in a situation where you need real, focused expertise. You need a plan and recommendations on how to accomplish the work. You may also need to know what others have done in similar circumstances and the results they received from their efforts. You may want to know in advance the probable obstacles you are likely to encounter and how to eliminate or mitigate them. If this sounds like a list of benefits and features you are searching for, you may need a consultant. We have had the privilege to work with globally renowned consulting firms and lesser-known niche groups. Both can add huge value. Our advice here is simple: Hire the best you can afford with the subject matter expertise you need. A good consultant will improve your final work product, accelerate your learning curve, increase your probability of success, and shorten the time required to complete the work.

Start a Leadership Development Group—Do you have a group of peers you consistently learn from? You can. Both of us are part of a group that began almost 30 years ago for the purpose of studying leadership. Now, some of you are thinking, *This section is supposed to contain ideas to help us find Fresh Eyes.* You are correct. One of the benefits of being in a group like the one we're describing is that relationships grow over time. These relationships foster trust. If there is trust, truth is not far behind.

Beyond studying leadership, we also share our annual development plans. In the process of creating these plans, we share our thoughts, hopes, dreams, and challenges. The next step is to solicit input on how we can best invest our developmental energy in the upcoming year. We even share the first draft of our plans for feedback. The comments are often direct and challenging. We can say from experience the group's perspective is always welcomed.

For a free PDF on how to start your own leadership development group, go to **https://leadeveryday.com/groups**, *or scan this QR code:*

PRACTICE!

Make a commitment to find Fresh Eyes! We'd love to hear what happens after you do. Please send us an email at **Info@LeadEveryDay.com**. We want to cheer you on!

Choice #2

GROW CAPACITY

Grow Capacity to meet the demands of the moment and the challenges of the future.

There is perhaps no greater frustration than to be a leader in quicksand due to a lack of capacity. This deficit can manifest itself emotionally, physically, relationally, or just be a shortfall in the time required to lead well.

We can both identify with this problem. There have been seasons in our lives and leadership when we have not had adequate capacity. Once, years ago, Mark's team had to resort to working seven days a week. Actually, it was worse than that. Sometimes, during this season, they would not go home for days. A short nap on the floor or a random sofa was the norm for a while. That's a real capacity problem. Fortunately, it was a season, not a lifestyle.

A couple of years ago, the two of us did 249 presentations in one year. This was clearly not sustainable. We've been on a journey ever since to grow our organizational capacity so we can serve more leaders and their organizations, not less. We understand the challenges of capacity.

We have added to the frustration for some leaders when we tell them the second choice to escape your quicksand is to Grow Capacity. To many, this feels like more than a challenge—they perceive it as delusional, a pure fantasy. We say, "Not at all!"

There are many ways to Grow Capacity: Defer work, delegate work, eliminate noncritical activities, redefine goals, set new timelines, automate what you can, outsource, modify your structure, muster more resources (people or money), clean up your calendar (every minute you save is a minute of capacity), improve your personal fitness, and more. The answers you seek may be a combination of these strategies. Not everything on this list is within your reach, but you probably don't think any of these ideas are absurd. Our next idea—the one we are going to go deeper on—may challenge you to think differently. The following is the only idea to Grow Capacity that is totally counterintuitive: Cultivate the leadership discipline of margin.

Pursue Margin

Let's begin by clarifying what margin is not. It's not taking the time to do email. Doing email is important but not the type of activity you should undertake in the spirit of margin. Margin is not going on vacation. We are huge fans of vacation, but that's not what we're talking about here. Margin is not taking a day off. Margin is a leadership discipline. Margin is the practice of routinely setting aside time for strategic, thoughtful work—a time to think about and address your most pressing issues, a time to wrestle with the inevitable trade-offs leaders must make.

Specifically, margin is a time to:

- **Reflect** on the past.
- **Assess** your current reality.
- **Create** your plans for the future.

Margin is so essential, yet, tragically, we meet too many leaders who say, "I don't have any time for those things." That is inexcusable. If the leaders are not engaged in these critical activities, who is? Who is leading your team or organization? When do you have time set aside to reflect, assess, and create? How much time do you set aside? How often? These are nontrivial questions because your efficacy as a leader hangs in the balance. Some will say, "Yes, I do that in the shower and during my commute." Your most pressing and complex issues will not be solved during your morning shower or rush-hour traffic. Leaders need time to think. This discipline is most likely our greatest contribution to the organizations we serve.

According to a 12-year study by Harvard, CEOs invested about 28% of their weekly working hours alone.[5] You may be wondering, "What are they doing?" Our best guess is they are reflecting, assessing, and creating.

A friend of ours became the president of a multibillion-dollar organization. When asked what he did first, he said he doubled the amount of time he allocated for margin. How much time do you need to invest? We don't know. What we do know is—the bigger your dreams, challenges, and obstacles, the more time you'll need.

Leaders throughout history have practiced this discipline. In his book *Leading Minds*, Howard Gardner shares examples of leaders who understood and practiced what he called a "Rhythm of Life," which included a dance of immersion (personal involvement) and isolation (margin). Famous practitioners include Margaret Mead, Albert Einstein, Eleanor Roosevelt, Winston Churchill, Sigmund Freud, Mahatma Gandhi, Abraham Lincoln, and Martin Luther King Jr.[6]

Since Mark published *Smart Leadership*, the most common questions regarding margin have been about the actual practice. Margin is such a foreign concept for so many leaders, we decided to go a little deeper here.

How to Maximize Margin

In addition to being a time to reflect, assess, and create, margin is also a time to focus. What do you focus on? You have options: the past, present, or future—perhaps all three.

To this statement, many leaders have asked, "Yes, but how do I structure my time?"

It depends. First, how much time do you have to invest? Second, how often do you schedule margin? As an example, if you have only one hour, you may need to invest your time on any current urgent issues. And if you have time scheduled weekly, you can feel more comfortable responding to a pressing issue because you'll have dedicated time set aside again in a few days. Hopefully, any urgent issue will be under control before your next session.

Let's say you have given yourself four hours for margin. You can build your agenda around the three primary activities outlined above. You could dedicate the first hour to *reflect* on a major project or event that occurred since you last practiced margin. You could ask questions such as:

- How successful was _____?
- What metrics am I basing my assessment on?
- What would we want to repeat if we did _____ again?
- What could have been improved?
- What did I do that hindered the work?
- What did I learn from the experience?

Next, turn your attention to your current reality. During this phase of your time, *assess* your current reality; identify any issues requiring your attention. Hopefully, you could work through several questions to determine next steps in the second hour. Obviously, this time allocation is *totally* based on the magnitude, complexity, and severity of the situation. If it is *huge*, you may need to dedicate more time to this issue. Here are some questions to consider. (A disclaimer: These are generic questions. The actual nature of the challenge will likely reveal better questions.)

- What is the root cause of the problem?
- What have others done successfully to respond to a similar situation?
- Who can help us solve this?
- What additional resources (leadership, financial, staffing, time, etc.) should we apply?
- What's our next step? Who will do what by when?

Once you've dedicated appropriate time and focus to what is urgent, you can turn your attention to the future. This is the *create* phase of your agenda. We think a good goal is to devote at least half your time in margin to the future. In this example, you would have approximately two hours for this portion of your agenda. There are an infinite number of questions you can ask about your future. Over time, we're guessing you'll come up with some favorites (if you don't already have them). Here are a few we really like:

- What do I want to be true in a decade that is not true today? You can change the time horizon as you wish. Just be sure to keep a sufficient focus on the future. If you don't, who will? You can also focus this question on a lengthy list of topics: your business, your team, your finances, your relationships, your health, and so on.
- What do I need to do in the next week, month, and year to move toward that reality?
- What will I need to do differently to make the future I envision a reality?
- What obstacles and barriers do I anticipate will slow or block my progress?
- How will I measure my progress?

We think you get the spirit of the exercise. What can we learn from our past experiences? What's happening today that needs my attention? What do we need to do differently going forward? If you allocate a few hours to periodically ask and answer questions like these, your impact will increase.

PRACTICE!

If you have not already discovered the miracle that is margin and made it part of your ongoing rhythm of life, schedule two hours next week, or the week after that, and begin to lead at a higher level. This is probably not the "right" amount of time. You'll have to discern that over time. Just get started.

*This is another topic we'd love to hear from you on. Send us an email with your questions and your breakthroughs as you begin to cultivate the ancient leadership discipline of margin to **Info@LeadEveryDay.com.***

Choice #3

FUEL CURIOSITY

Fuel Curiosity to maintain relevance and vitality in a changing world.

Is there a leadership fountain of youth? In the past, our response to this question was, "We hope so because we want to add value for the rest of our lives." Now, we can definitively say, "Yes!" Curiosity is the leader's ticket to a lifetime of contribution. You'll also be glad to know curiosity plays a critical role in helping you escape the quicksand and increase your impact.

Have you ever wondered why more leaders don't practice curiosity? We have. We think the primary reason is the quicksand. When a leader finds themselves in the quagmire, curiosity is probably one of the last things on their mind. This is just one more reason you need to escape and make your way to solid ground.

Ask, Don't Tell

Twenty years ago, Mark spent a couple of months in Boston attending Harvard's Advanced Management Program. His group completed more than 100 case studies over eight weeks. One of the cases focused on two global incidents from the 1960s—the Bay of Pigs and the Cuban Missile Crisis. Both of these occurred on the watch of President John F. Kennedy.

Shortly after taking office, President Kennedy learned of a planned US mission to incite and support a revolution in Cuba. The plan had been developed by the CIA during Eisenhower's term in office. Although the plan was based on several false assumptions, the CIA had garnered the support of senior military leaders. The most egregious misstep was likely the decision not to include input from the State Department leaders assigned to Latin America. Those favoring the invasion were so outspoken, including the Joint Chiefs of Staff, that no one on Kennedy's team opposed the plan although many doubts about its viability and probability of success persisted.[7]

On April 17, 1961, the main invasion landed on the beach at the Bay of Pigs. The landing was met with fierce opposition from local militia. The president responded by withdrawing US air support. This decision sealed the fate of the mission. The insurgents were routed, and all were killed or captured. Castro leveraged this victory to further his image as a heroic leader and create an even stronger bond with the Soviets.

In the days following the embarrassing defeat, the president commissioned a review of foreign-policy decision-making and instituted several changes. In the future, the process would shift from advocacy to inquiry. As it turned out, this would be a good thing for the world.

In October 1962, the United States learned the Soviets had placed nuclear missiles in Cuba, which presented a clear threat to American security. The president assembled many of the same players who had been through the Bay of Pigs fiasco. This time, their approach was fundamentally different. It was not about advocating a position; it was focused on exploring options and asking the right questions. The team worked for two weeks, ultimately giving the president two viable options: a surgical airstrike or a total blockade of the island nation. He chose the latter. In this superpower staring match, the Soviets blinked and removed their missiles and bombers on November 20, 1962.[8]

There is a lot we could process from these two situations. What can you learn from this case? Are you more inclined to advocate for your position as opposed to asking enough questions to learn the points of view held by others? When you learn to ask more than tell, you'll enjoy several benefits:

- You'll get smarter.
- The group will get smarter.
- You'll create more engagement and buy-in to the ultimate solution.
- You'll make better decisions.
- Your results will improve.

Here are a few ideas to help you ask better questions.

Open-ended questions will root out more information. Many leaders prefer to ask yes/no questions. These closed-ended questions aren't devoid of value, but they leave a lot to be desired. Another form of closed-ended questions are the ones that can be answered with a single word. Rather than ask your child, "How was your day?" to which they will likely say, "Fine," try this: "What was your favorite part of your day?" If they say, "Lunch," the follow-up question might be, "What made lunch so enjoyable?"

Don't be afraid to ask questions no one knows the answers to.
One of the more challenging ideas we've encountered regarding questions pertains to the topic or issue no one knows the answer to. For example, "If what you just described doesn't work, what will we do next?" Or, "What are the implications if our key assumption is invalid?" You don't ask these questions just to be a contrarian. You ask them to help the group think and plan for an uncertain future. In many cases, you'll discover the question no one knows the answer to is the most valuable question you can ask.

PRACTICE!

Make a list of your current top 10 questions and work to add at least one question per week. Look for every opportunity to put one of your questions to work. The dividends will most likely surprise you. This growing list will become an inflation-proof investment that will compound exponentially over the course of your career.

Choice #4

CREATE CHANGE

Create Change today to ensure a better tomorrow.

How successful are you at leading change? Why is this question relevant? We meet far too many leaders who think change is a burden, a nuisance, an obstacle to be avoided, or something to be dreaded. These leaders don't understand leadership. Our *job* is to create and sustain positive change in service of the vision or mission of the organization we serve. Uncommon Leaders also understand that progress is always preceded by change. No change, no progress.

What do you need to change to improve your effectiveness? By this point, we hope the connection between this choice to Create Change and the previous three choices is clear. These choices were never intended to represent a nice, neat, sequential process map. However, there is a deep interdependency here.

If you don't Confront Reality, Grow Capacity, and Fuel Your Curiosity, it is unlikely you will be able to create the necessary changes. One disclaimer is also in order: Activating the first three choices does not guarantee you'll make the needed changes. To Create Change is a separate choice, and in many ways, the most critical. Here's why: Your current systems, structure, beliefs, and behaviors are perfectly aligned to give you the output you are now receiving. If you don't change something, the chances of anything improving are slim to none. Remember, different is not always better, but better is always different.

Some leaders hope things will get better. They hope for increased sales, growing profits, new levels of achievement with customer satisfaction and employee retention. Let us know how this approach works out for you.

Hope is not a strategy.

If you want different outcomes, what are you willing to change?

All this talk about change surfaces a real problem: Change is incredibly difficult. Worse than that, although the data is a bit hard to come by, conventional wisdom is that 70% of change efforts fail. Yes, seven out of ten times when a leader institutes a change, it will fail. Our own global change study revealed that frontline contributors have a more morose view of change.[9] They contend that large-scale change efforts actually decrease employee engagement. In other words, the organization is worse off after the effort ends. This worsening is perhaps due to leadership's failure to admit the failure of the change effort (leaders tend to have a more favorable view of the outcomes than their workforce).

We don't share any of this to give you permission to throw up your hands and say, "Well, I guess I should take change out of my playbook." No! Your entire playbook is about change. Your vision is about a preferred future. When you engage and develop others, you are helping people change. To Reinvent Continuously is totally about change. We assume you see the pattern here. Finally, you will not escape the quicksand unless you change something. So, what do you do?

Leading Successful Change

As we reflect on our careers to date, the most difficult and frustrating work has involved Creating Change. Mark recalls one large-scale change project he worked on for more than a decade with only a fraction of the success he envisioned. Why is it so hard? It's hard because leading change has much in common with juggling.

Some of you reading this can juggle. Congratulations! If you can, you know a few things: You *learned* how to juggle. The process of learning was time-consuming. And, even on your best days, you will still drop a ball. When you do drop a ball, you don't quit juggling. You work to improve your skills.

While conducting our research on change, we interviewed a juggler from the world-renowned Cirque du Soleil. He provided deep insight into the challenges we intuitively assumed. He also underscored our core belief around the difficulty of the activity. He said in a typical routine he drops the ball three to five times. This is a man who has dedicated his life to his craft. As you attempt to lead change, from time to time, you will drop the ball. You must maintain your composure, pick up the ball(s), and keep juggling. By the way, the more balls you want to juggle, the more you'll need to practice—and with more balls and more practice come more drops.[10]

As leaders, how can we improve this essential skill set of leading change so we drop fewer balls? You can guess our response—practice!

In the balance of this chapter, we'll share our initial high-level findings from a recent multimillion-dollar research project in which we were attempting to understand what the best leaders do in the arena of change in hopes of learning from their example. Many of our "discoveries" will certainly reinforce what you already know about leading change; please consider these thoughts as a friendly reminder. Then, we'll close with what may be a new idea for you. We'll focus on the single greatest factor impacting your efficacy as an agent of change.

Let's start with the obvious. To successfully lead a complex change, a leader must embrace several key elements that are absolutely essential regardless of the change you are attempting to create.

Communication—In some of the literature on change, this is often inadequately described as vision. Yes, the vision is critical but insufficient. Ongoing communication will be the lifeblood of your change efforts. People need to be apprised of the progress of the change effort, including setbacks and lessons learned.

Support—Support includes the usual suspects: training, tools, recognition, staffing, encouragement, technology, metrics, coaching, and in some cases, restructuring or reassigning work to make way for the new and improved.

Energy—Providing the energy for change is a role leadership is uniquely positioned to play. The problem is most organizations have too many change efforts in play at any one time for the leader to provide all the energy. Therefore, in most complex change efforts, additional leaders must be deputized to keep the flame of change burning.

Experimentation—As we studied those leaders and organizations where change efforts were more successful, a theme emerged regarding what some called iteration. For now, we're calling it experimentation. Virtually all large-scale change efforts begin with a plan (most medium-sized ones do too). Our research revealed an ever-present willingness to adjust the plan and try new things along the way. We even saw ample situations where leadership changed the destination based on the lessons they were learning as their change efforts played out in real time.

Communication, support, energy, and experimentation. This list may appear complete, but there is one more essential ingredient. One that surprised our team.

What differentiates those leaders and organizations who have a much higher success rate at leading change? We call it Dynamic Awareness. What is it, and why does it matter?

Maintain Dynamic Awareness

Dynamic Awareness is the ability to survey a wide field of activities simultaneously, understand the short- and longer-term implications of your observations, and determine the most appropriate next step. A leader practicing Dynamic Awareness in the context of a change initiative is able to see the gaps and opportunities impeding progress toward the desired future and identify the necessary course corrections.

Why is Dynamic Awareness such a critical skill? The nature of change has changed. With all due respect to John Kotter, esteemed professor at the Harvard Business School, and his eight-step linear change process, we now live in a nonlinear world. The days of the Step One, Step Two, Step Three approach to change are gone.

Today, what is required is a leader who can communicate the initial vision, provide resources, go back and communicate the vision again, deputize more leaders to infuse additional energy, provide more support, update the organization on the status of the change, experiment with new methods to better embed the change, cast the vision again, recognize those making progress, provide support, and on and on and on. Notice the pattern of activity? You are correct—there is no pattern! This is the new world of successful change efforts. Every change is uncharted water. To navigate safely to your destination requires a leader with Dynamic Awareness.

How are you doing with the idea of Dynamic Awareness? We know it's a new term, but think about a recent or current change effort. Spend a few minutes reflecting on the status of the change. Are you on track? Have your efforts stalled?

Here are three questions you can ask to increase your Dynamic Awareness:

- What's happening?
- Why is it happening?
- What should we do next?

In the beginning, these questions will seem forced. Over time, if you persist, they will become second nature. Remember, the nature of *change* has changed. You will need a new way to assess your change efforts in real time; it's no longer enough to create the plan and run the play.

As you ask yourself the above questions, you'll need to constantly filter what you are experiencing through the lens of the other conditions required for successful change: communications, support, energy, and experimentation. Your next steps will be contained in one or more of these elements. Here's an example. When you see people who have obviously not embraced the desired change by the behaviors you see them exhibiting, you need to ask and answer the next diagnostic question: "What is happening?"

Your answer could be any number of things: Maybe they don't understand the new behavior. Is their supervisor encouraging them (i.e., providing the needed energy for the change)? Perhaps they have not yet been trained—this would be an issue of support. Who knows? Maybe they don't have the tools yet. Could the problem be they've been trying the new method for months and it doesn't produce the desired result? If this is the case, your next step may need to be experimentation.

PRACTICE!

Start using the three diagnostic questions from the previous page immediately as you assess the current state of any change initiative. You'll be able to more easily and accurately identify your best next steps.

For bonus points, teach your leaders the concept of Dynamic Awareness. Ask them to constantly ask and answer the three questions.

SO WHAT?

As we said previously, you get no credit for doing the wrong things with excellence. If you are in survival mode necessitated by the quicksand you inhabit on a daily basis, you are *not* doing the right things. Also, if you are attempting to swim in quicksand, you can't help those around you extricate themselves. You most likely don't have the time, energy, or expertise to free them. The consequences of your inaction have a ripple effect. Not only have you limited your effectiveness, but your inability to serve those around you seals their fate as well. You can ultimately end up with an entire team, department, or organization mired in mediocrity.

The good news is: You can escape the quicksand! Then you can help your team do the same. Begin today by putting the four Smart Choices to work and take your leadership, your team, and your organization to the higher, solid ground. From there, the sky's the limit!

Be smart!

Lead Every Day Operating System

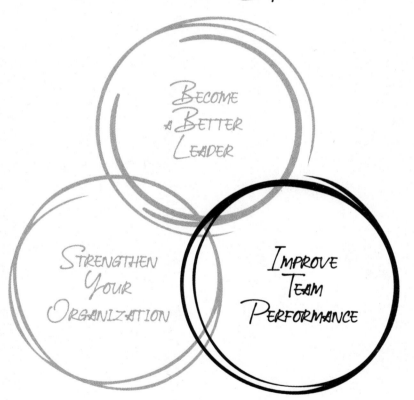

Become a Better Leader

Strengthen Your Organization

Improve Team Performance

IMPROVE TEAM PERFORMANCE

Individually, we are one drop. Together, we are an ocean.
—Ryunosuke Satoro

Teams built the pyramids, painted the ceiling of the Sistine Chapel (Michelangelo supervised 13 assistants), put men on the moon, harnessed the power of the atom, and built the iPhone. Teams, led well, not only outperform individuals, but they push the boundaries of what is thought possible. Because of the power inherent in a well-led team, much of the work in the world is organized and executed by teams. To thrive in today's dynamic environment, leaders must learn how to Improve Team Performance. This is the second discipline in our Lead Every Day Operating System.

Our team experiences began as small kids—we both participated in many different sports. Altogether, we played baseball, tennis, football, golf, basketball, softball, and Mark even dabbled in Ultimate Frisbee. Although we share many common memories from those formative years, our paths definitely diverged—Randy was on several amazing teams; Mark, not so much.

Even though we experienced varying degrees of success in our early team endeavors, what we didn't realize at the time is that these teams played a crucial role in shaping our lives far beyond sports. They laid the groundwork for how we collaborate with others, cope with setbacks, and much more. While we both gained valuable lessons through years of coaching and leading exceptional teams, there was a pivotal moment in Mark's career that truly elevated his understanding regarding the potential of a team.

In the late '80s, Chick-fil-A was looking to help the men and women who operated the company's restaurants improve quality. For those old enough to remember the 1980s, Total Quality Management (TQM) was all the rage. The principles and practices of statistical process control were transforming businesses, industries, and the global economy. Some organizations, like Toyota, were pursuing Six Sigma—this translated to only 3.4 defects per million opportunities![1]

After some investigation, Mark's team determined that even with the power and potential of these innovative approaches to quality improvement, they were too complex for an hourly workforce comprised predominantly of teenagers with turnover rates approaching 100%. However, at the heart of the quality revolution was an idea that they believed was undervalued and underdeveloped—teams.

The moment is still clear in his mind. His boss, Dan Cathy, who would eventually become CEO, walked into his office and offered a simple imperative: "Make us a team-based organization." Without waiting for a response, he turned and walked out, leaving Mark with a directive that would shape the next two decades of his career. While he took on other projects along the way, that assignment—building a team-based culture—was never far from his mind.

WHAT'S YOUR EXPERIENCE WITH TEAMS?

Let's be honest, most teams are dysfunctional. They waste time, energy, and effort. This is true in sports, businesses, nonprofit organizations, health care, schools, churches, and more. Have you ever wondered why this is the case? We've invested decades pondering this question. One of our conclusions: There are really three types of teams.

Underperformers—Teams that deplete resources with little or nothing positive to show for their efforts. Calling them Underperformers is probably generous. As we said above, most teams are dysfunctional and fall into this category.

Good Teams—These are teams that produce some results but never really set the world on fire. Their performance is adequate. No one is thrilled to be on these teams. Their greatest reward is a participation trophy.

High Performance Teams—These are teams that mystify others with their accomplishments. They create and sustain elite levels of performance. Often their results are exponentially better than the merely Good Teams. Once we discovered this universe, we became obsessed with discovering its secrets.

THE SECRET OF TEAMS

After more than a decade of discovery and application, Chick-fil-A decided it was time to document what they had learned about High Performance Teams—more specifically, it was Mark's new boss who gave him the assignment. He had been a huge advocate and contributor to the project to study great teams. He also knew the countless hours Mark's team had invested over more than a decade. Mark remembers the moment clearly. His boss asked, "Can you write a book on teams?"

Mark responded, "I think so."

"Good. We need it by February" (the date of the company's annual event).

The result was a book entitled *The Secret of Teams* in which they were able to distill all they'd learned down to a few essential behaviors. After this quick introduction, we'll devote the next several chapters to helping you operationalize some immutable practices you can use to help you build your own High Performance Team.

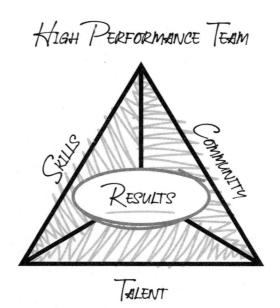

WHAT DO HIGH PERFORMANCE TEAMS DO?

Attract Top Talent. Talent doesn't guarantee your success. However, its absence can certainly doom you to mediocrity, or worse. The team with the best players does have the best *chance* to win. What's your plan to attract, select, and retain the best people? How well is your plan working? Talent is the foundation of High Performance Teams.

Master Team Basics. There are some simple, yet profound things the best teams consistently do. We call these the Basics. In the upcoming chapter, we'll look at seven team-altering practices that will transform your team. So we don't leave you hanging, here's a preview. Our list includes clarifying roles and goals, establishing an accompanying scorecard, conducting high-impact meetings, and more. We'll also talk about the critical role of team skills such as goal setting, problem-solving, facilitation, and conflict resolution. Skills like these multiply talent and turn aspirations into accomplishments.

Build Genuine Community. If the previous list of skills and team behaviors leaves you wanting, your instincts are correct. Top Talent and Team Basics are essential but insufficient if you want to breathe the rare air of High Performance Teams. The most successful teams in the world have created a place where people care about each other as much as they care about the work itself. We call this type of environment *community*. Community is the missing ingredient for many teams left unfulfilled by their meager results and participation trophy.

We want to make a prediction: Once you've been part of a true High Performance Team, you'll invest the rest of your career trying to protect and enhance the one you've created. And, if you ever leave this team, you'll invest the balance of your working years to create your next one. High Performance Teams are life-giving, soul-enriching performance machines. We're excited to help you build your very own. Let's get started!

ATTRACT TOP TALENT

Great vision without great people is irrelevant.
—Jim Collins

Late one night, Mark found himself in an unexpected meeting with the soon-to-be-named president of Chick-fil-A and the head of operations, where he learned about a challenge that would stretch him and expand his understanding of leadership.

For many years, the organization surveyed their key leaders asking them a familiar set of questions, including: What is the biggest challenge you are currently facing? What is the biggest challenge corporate could help you address? The senior leader asked Mark if he had seen the latest results of their annual leadership survey. He had not.

The answers had become as familiar as the questions; top issues always included items such as sales, profits, increasing government regulations, and so on. And, somewhere in the top 10, you could always count on seeing "finding and keeping people." However, this year was different. For the first time in the organization's history, the challenge of finding and keeping people had catapulted to the top spot on the list.

Mark left the room with the assignment to help the Operators solve this problem. Because many of the local restaurants relied heavily on a teenage workforce, there was inherent turnover. If an employee was struggling in school, it was common for their parents to tell them to reduce their hours or quit outright. If someone made the football team or cheerleading squad, they might leave as well. Not to mention those who would leave for college. All of this put extraordinary pressure on the individual restaurant. The war for talent, as it is often referred to, had arrived at Chick-fil-A's doorstep.

Reflecting on the moment, Mark recalled his initial reaction: "This is a Human Resources issue." At the time, he and his team were focused on leadership challenges. But within a few hours, reality set in. While HR could assist with problems like this, he quickly realized that finding and retaining people was undeniably a chief responsibility of leadership.

Before assembling the team that would ultimately help tackle this problem, Mark went to see a veteran Operator who had a stellar reputation for attracting great people. He wanted as much clarity as possible on this critical issue before the team began its work. As Mark laid out the challenge as he understood it, he received the insight that would change the direction of this work and the destiny of tens of thousands of organizations around the world.

"You don't understand the problem," Mark's host said.

"Well, I think we do. We're trying to figure out how to help leaders find and keep people."

"That's not the problem," the wise leader patiently offered.

"Okay, I'm here to learn from you. But do you know what the data says?"

"You asked the wrong question. Getting more people is not the challenge; we could significantly increase our starting wage and have folks lined up for an interview."

"So, what's the real problem?" Mark asked sheepishly.

"How do you attract and keep the *right* people? That's the challenge. That's the problem you need to solve."

This conversation changed everything. First, the team had to differentiate the *right* people from the *almost* right people. They rightly concluded that most leaders could easily identify the *wrong* people, so they wouldn't spend any time or energy on this.

They ultimately chose the term Top Talent for the right people. Who are they? They are your "A" players. They are the people you would hate to lose. We called the almost-right players Typical Talent—good, but not outstanding. Next, we began to search for existing research on the topic of attracting Top Talent. This was the most frustrating season of this multiyear project. We invested six months and yet couldn't find any research to answer our question.

We talked to global HR firms, we talked to academics, we even called Marcus Buckingham, then with the Gallup organization. Every call ended with the same conclusion: No one had ever conducted the research we were seeking. "Why not?" Mark asked. The response was unanimous: "Finding the answer would be time-consuming, extremely difficult, and very expensive."

This left the team with no choice but to do the work themselves. They knew they would have to get inside the heads and hearts of both Top Talent and Typical Talent to understand why they made the decisions they did about where they would work. They went back to one of those big HR organizations and wrote them a huge check to help us answer the question: What is Top Talent looking for when seeking a job?

After surveying thousands, interviewing and conducting numerous focus groups with hundreds more, their total sample encompassed more than 7,000 participants ages 15–65+, representing all 50 states. Thanks to that team, we now know what Top Talent wants and wrote about our findings in *Talent Magnet*.[1]

Here, we'll share a summary of what they learned and what you can begin to do today to create your own Talent Magnet. Top Talent wants—no, they demand—three things: a Better Boss, a

Brighter Future, and a Bigger Vision. This is the value proposition that will attract and keep these talented individuals.

BETTER BOSS

The first conclusion the data revealed is Top Talent wants a Better Boss. In other words, they want to be well-led. Now, having shared this content widely for a few years, we know what some of you are thinking: *Doesn't everyone want to be led well?* At some level, yes, but for Top Talent this is a condition of employment. If these most talented individuals discover they are not going to have a good leader, they are an immediate flight risk. Typical Talent will grumble and complain about their boss, but they will usually stay. Here's something all leaders need to remember: Top Talent has options—they do not have to stay with you. Every organization is looking for these individuals. Don't give them a reason to leave; give them ample reasons to stay on your team.

What does it mean to be a Better Boss? That is certainly a non-trivial question. A Better Boss is:

An engaged, caring individual who can meet the leadership demands of the moment and the demands of an unknown future.

How's that for a job description? Let's face it, as leaders we have chosen an incredibly challenging profession. Fortunately, the rewards outweigh the difficulties . . . on most days.

The pursuit of mastery in leadership is a lifelong quest. You could argue this entire book is a response to the call to become a Better Boss. But in the spirit of providing you an Operating System and tangible next steps, we suggest every leader on the planet should have an Individual Development Plan (IDP) focused on their own improvement as a leader.

Create a Plan

Leaders, perhaps more than any other profession, understand the power of a plan. You have plans for your organization, your sales growth and market expansion, marketing, quality improvement, strategic plans, operating plans, plans for innovation, and personal financial plans. We are baffled by how few leaders have a plan for their personal growth and development. The bottom line, as stated by Tim Tassopoulos, former president of Chick-fil-A: "If you want your organization to grow by 10% next year, *you* had better grow by at least 10%." Organizations cannot outgrow their leadership.

In light of these realities, the small number of leaders who are thinking strategically about their growth is maddening. Most leaders are smart people. What's the disconnect? We're tempted to share the top 10 reasons most leaders don't have an Individual Development Plan. However, if you don't have one yet, you know why you don't. If you do have one, congratulations! If you actually use your plan to guide your growth and development (some leaders create them and just file them away), you are among a very small group of leaders who are stewarding their talent and consciously creating more capacity for their future.

If you don't currently have a plan and are tempted to skip this section, please don't! You are at risk on two fronts—one, you lack the moral authority to ask others to take their personal growth seriously. Two, you are in jeopardy of falling prey to arrogance, hubris, and irrelevance. As Marshall Goldsmith famously declared, "What got you here won't get you there." The best leaders are learners, and a plan is a great tool to facilitate your continuing growth.[2]

How do you begin? Is there a template? We have long shunned the idea of a template. Everyone is different. Every plan should be created to meet the needs and preferences of the individual leader. We have known leaders with IDPs that were 30 pages in length and others who have written them on a napkin, both with equal impact! Your plan must work for you.

Here are some tips and guidelines that will be helpful as you work to create your plan.

Learn from Your Past. Every year we sit down in the fall and ask ourselves a series of questions. These questions are our first line of defense to ensure we'll invest our time and resources on the right developmental topics in the upcoming year. Here are some starter questions for you to consider:

- What did you learn in the last year that has implications for your upcoming plan?
- What disciplines/activities/practices work best for you when attempting to grow?
- What was the greatest hindrance to your growth during the past year?
- How will you identify gaps and blind spots in your life and leadership?
- What are your learning style preferences (reading, relationships, experiences, etc.)?
- What could you have done better in the past to accelerate your growth and contribution?
- Do you currently have any critical gaps related to your core responsibilities? (This is a question you really can't answer by yourself. You'll need others to help here.)
- Which of your strengths could you better leverage through continued intentional development?

Don't waste your past. As Howard Hendricks, one of Mark's

mentors, famously said, "Experience is not the best teacher—evaluated experience is."

Learn from your past, but don't live there.

Focus Your Development. Let's face it, all of us have unlimited areas where we could grow. Most leaders want to be more fit, a better communicator, more strategic, more empathetic, more persuasive, and better listeners. The list of options is endless. The temptation is to attempt to do too much. We have limited time and energy to invest in our development. If we pursue too many topics, we dilute our resources and as a result we may not see any growth. Chris McChesney in the *4 Disciplines of Execution* says we should all focus on a few "Wildly Important Goals." He suggests this approach will yield a far superior outcome than shooting for the moon.[3] Our recommendation is to choose one or two areas for improvement.

Go back to the questions above; a thoughtful answer to each of them should give you direction, if not clarity, on where you should target your development efforts.

Write It Down. A written plan is infinitely more valuable than one that exists in your mind alone. Once your plan is documented, you can more easily share it with others. You'll also find a written plan significantly easier to review and use to track your performance. When you put your plan on paper (or in your computer), and are specific, you'll also find your execution will increase dramatically.

Find a Mentor. Although the strategies and tactics you can employ to grow are virtually limitless, we feel strongly that every leader should have a mentor, or perhaps more than one, helping you on your journey. Some leaders don't have a mentor because they've not found the perfect fit. Don't set the bar too high. After you know what you're trying to accomplish, the goal is to find someone who is farther up the development curve who is willing to help you grow. (For a review of a few additional ideas, go back to page 72.)

Apply Your Learning. Some leaders are so excited about learning, they forget about the doing. They miss that learning is not the goal but rather an enabler of greater contribution and value we can bring to those we serve. Given how most adults learn, actually applying the things you are learning accelerates and solidifies real growth. Look for opportunities to incorporate the doing in your plan. As an example, if you are working to become a better public speaker, set a goal around how many talks you want to give in the upcoming year.

Share Your Plan. This is a big deal. According to a study by the Association for Talent Development (ATD), individuals who commit to someone else about their goals have a 65% chance of completing them. Even more striking, those who establish regular accountability check-ins with someone have a 95% chance of success in achieving their goals.[4]

We have a group of people we share our annual plans with (we've been doing this for decades). When you do, you'll have some additional accountability to execute the plan. You can also use this group as a source of input when creating future plans. Do you have a small group of trusted friends and colleagues you could share your plan with? If not, you may want to begin cultivating such a group. (For some practical tips, go back and review page 73.)

Review Your Plan. Maybe this is too obvious to include on our list. If you invest the time to create a plan, we're sure you will use it to guide your activities. Maybe. Busyness and distractions are the enemy. One way to combat the day-to-day pressure pushing your personal growth and development to the fringes is to review your plan often. Mark has created a one-page summary of his plan—his goal is to review it daily. Regardless of the frequency you choose, the self-accountability this practice fosters will help you execute your plan at a higher level.

┌─ PRACTICE! ─────────────────────────────

What is your plan for personal and professional growth? If you don't already have a plan, make this a top priority. Write it down.

If you'd like a free development plan template, go to **https://lead everyday.com/plan-template**, *or scan this QR code:*

BRIGHTER FUTURE

The next thing Top Talent wants in a job is a Brighter Future. Okay, we can hear the question: *Doesn't everyone want a Brighter Future?* Not exactly. For Typical Talent, the future is Friday. Top Talent has a much longer time horizon. When they consider accepting a spot on your team, they are asking a different set of questions. They are definitely asking themselves: *How will this job or role prepare me for the future? What will I learn in the role? How will I be stretched?*

A *Harvard Business Review* study found that 76% of high performers believe that opportunities for growth and development are one of the top reasons for staying at a company.[5] According to Pew Research Center, 63% of workers that left their job cited no opportunity for advancement as the reason for leaving.[6]

Top Talent expects to grow, and they expect the organizations they join to help them. We've talked to leaders who don't like this finding. We understand. But don't forget, Top Talent has choices. If they don't work for you, there are tens of thousands of other companies willing to hire them.

Champion Growth

Are you a Champion for Growth? If 10 people who work with you were asked to describe you, how many would say anything vaguely related to this concept? Do you care deeply about the growth and development of your people? If so, how has your concern manifested itself in systems and processes to institutionalize personal growth? How much does your organization invest in programming for development? Would others in your industry describe your organization as a learning organization? All of these answers should provide clues regarding the current state of affairs. If you have room for improvement here, the following ideas should be helpful.

Model Lifelong Learning. Are you a learner? Do you share what you're learning with others? One of Mark's mentors challenged him with the idea of being a running stream for those around him, not a stagnant pool. You have that same choice. Besides, if you want to continue to grow your impact, influence, and opportunity, lifelong learning is the only path. Your capacity to grow will determine your capacity to lead.

Invest in Development. As a leader, there is a good chance you have some discretion regarding how money is allocated in your organization or even at the team level. Is professional development an unfunded mandate? What message are you sending intentionally or subconsciously based on how you fund development? If someone wanted to attend a conference aligned with their development plan, would they have access to the funding? If someone needed an outside coach to help elevate their performance, would this investment have to be a personal expense? If someone was interested in going back to school, would your organization help? How you invest your time and dollars can magnify or undermine your status as a Champion for Growth.

Require Individual Development Plans (IDP). Does your organization require employees to have an annual plan for the work they are accountable for completing? Depending on the nature of your organization, you may require business plans from various entities in your portfolio. Expense reports have due dates each month. Nonexempt employees are required to submit their hours for approval and payment. None of this sounds out of the ordinary, does it? If you make a list of what is required in your organization, it could be a long list. What is typically not required is a development plan. This is a missed opportunity.

Teams we've led and organizations we've served have embraced the practice of IDPs for decades. The plan is co-created and approved by the employee's supervisor. Then, periodically, there can be a check-in to determine progress and offer assistance. If you do this single activity, your stock as a Champion for Growth will skyrocket.

Celebrate Growth. One of our favorite quotes is from Plato: "What is honored in a country is cultivated there."[7] The same principle applies in the modern organization and on your team. If you want more growth, honor those who are growing. Recognize their efforts and their accomplishments. Has someone recently completed an advanced degree? Have people on your team been invited to speak at conferences and industry events? Ask team members to share what they are learning in a team setting. Activities like these accelerate growth and development.

> ## PRACTICE!
> Identify any current activities you believe stimulate growth and others that could send mixed or negative messages. Meet with your team and create a plan to accelerate growth.

BIGGER VISION

The third thing Top Talent wants that is less important to Typical Talent is the opportunity to contribute to something bigger than themselves. This desire doesn't necessarily mean just something bigger, such as a bigger organization. Think about the cause, the contribution, and the impact the organization is having on a larger scale. Is your organization a force for good in the world? Nothing in our data indicated these most talented people didn't care about traditional success metrics like shareholder value or profits; they just wanted more. They are people who really do want to make a difference as much as they want to make a living.

Some may see this and think this is a newfangled idea of those "young people." No, that's not what the data indicates. One reason we included people from ages 15–65+ is that we wanted to test for generational differences. Top Talent across all demographics wants to be part of a Bigger Vision. A deeper look revealed that, yes, this was about contribution, but it was also an indicator of a deep-seated desire for the organization's leadership to be thoughtful and strategic. The mere presence of vision, purpose, mission, and the like was more important to Top Talent. This finding underscores their desire to be well-led.

Ensure Alignment

Alignment is one of the more challenging tasks a leader will encounter over the course of a career. Many factors converge to conspire against it. Some of the usual suspects include misaligned leaders, lack of or poor communication, mixed messages, distractions, turnover, job rotations, changing leadership, busyness, competing priorities, resource scarcity, and sometimes the volume of work itself can hinder alignment. Does all of this sound a lot like quicksand?

Therefore, before we proceed, we want to acknowledge the enormity of the challenge and that our Yes, but How? admonition stated in two simple words, Ensure Alignment, doesn't begin to convey the magnitude of effort that will be required.

Hopefully, we've established the fact that this is a big task with huge consequences. And to be clear, alignment is bigger than the vision required to attract and retain Top Talent. Alignment is one of the four moves all High Performance Organizations make. In that context, we call it Act as One. We'll do a deeper dive into this topic in an upcoming chapter on Strengthening Your Organization. For now, here are a few ideas to help you begin the never-ending quest for alignment.

Select for Alignment. Assuming you have a Bigger Vision for your organization, one grounded in a clear aspiration, use this in your interview and selection process. By the way, your aspiration can be expressed in a number of ways. Some of the most common mechanisms include purpose, vision, mission, values, and ethos. Are you selecting people who will struggle to align or are you selecting people who will embrace what you are trying to accomplish and add value to the cause?

One of our favorite examples is from a leader who was trying to build a customer-centric organization. He shared the story of a final interview with a promising candidate. As we heard this story, we created our own image of the candidate. He was bright, articulate, and had a firm handshake and a warm smile. During the interview, the conversation turned to the prospective candidate's previous job. At this point he revealed how much he loved his former job except for one thing—he said he hated the customers. You can decide how you think this story ended. Here's our question for you: Are you selecting mission-capable people? How much effort will be required to get a new person aligned? The right answer is "as little as possible."

Onboard Well. Once you've made a good hire, your work to align this new person is only beginning. Unfortunately, many people neglect this crucial step in the alignment process. Let's pause and clarify terms here. Orientation is different from onboarding.

Orientation is typically an administrative process in which the new employee signs some papers, is given a key to the building and/or a security card, and is briefed on numerous policies. In the days when people went to a physical office, new folks would be given a tour, including the lunchroom, the mail room, and the restrooms. You can make the case that all of this was/is needed.

However, onboarding is an enculturation process. This is where you take the next step to impart and implant the DNA of the organization into the hearts and minds of your newest team members. Who owns this step in the alignment process in your organization? When was the last time you attended a full onboarding session? You may decide to periodically schedule your team to go back through the onboarding process to reinforce your cultural DNA.

Communicate Strategically. Apples fall from trees, water flows downhill, and vision leaks. Gallup's "State of the American Workplace" report indicates that only about 41% of employees strongly agree that they know what their company stands for and what makes it different from competitors.[8]

Regardless of how carefully you select vision- and mission-aligned people and no matter how thorough and complete their onboarding, the factors mentioned earlier still conspire 24/7 to move an organization toward misalignment. One of your best tools to combat the slide is strategic communications.

This topic is far beyond the scope of this book. However, please don't leave messaging to chance. Someone needs to be accountable, whether in a full-time, part-time, or project assignment role, to ensure key messages surrounding your vision are crafted and communicated well. Whoever owns this responsibility will also need to think carefully about the messengers, methods, and frequency. The fatal flaw is to assume that because the vision was mentioned at your annual event three years ago, everyone knows the vision and supports it wholeheartedly. That's not going to happen.

A study from the *Journal of Consumer Research* found that a message typically needs to be heard seven times before it fully sinks in with an audience. This is often referred to as the "Rule of Seven" in marketing and communication strategy. The implications for leaders as we attempt to align the people in our organization: We are going to have to repeat the key messages again and again.[9]

> ## PRACTICE!
>
> Ask your team members to identify any areas where they perceive misalignment between your employee value proposition (Better Boss, Brighter Future, and Bigger Vision) and reality. There are a number of ways to do this. Consider individual conversations, focus groups, or an anonymous survey. You may want to do all three. Once you have clarity on your opportunity areas, get to work.

TELL YOUR STORY

There's one more thing we need to address. The data was clear—Top Talent wants three things: to be well-led (a Better Boss), to learn and grow (a Brighter Future), and to be part of something bigger than themselves (a Bigger Vision). So, imagine our surprise when, during the final phase of our work, some leaders started pushing back. Not just mild disagreement—some of the most skilled and experienced leaders we knew said outright our model was flawed. In fact, they claimed it didn't work at all.

At first, we were puzzled. But after asking a lot of questions, we stumbled upon an insight. These leaders claimed they were offering exactly what Top Talent wanted, yet they still struggled to attract the right people. The more we dug into their stories, the more we realized they were missing a crucial element. Even if you provide everything Top Talent is looking for, it won't matter if you don't Tell the Story.

When we explored this further, we discovered that the timing and content of the story were just as important as the message itself. One leader, for example, shared how he told his Better Boss,

Brighter Future, and Bigger Vision story during orientation—but at that point, the message was ineffective for *attracting* Top Talent. The employees were already on his payroll.

Another leader had a different issue. He was proactive, telling the company's story to potential recruits. The problem? He was telling the *wrong* story. His focus was on the company's history—great material for orientation, but it wasn't the story Top Talent wanted to hear.

Deputize Everyone

As you can imagine, there is a lot you can do to Tell the Story. Our recommendation is to tell the *right* story as many ways as possible. The "war for talent" is a phrase McKinsey consultants coined in 1997.[10] More than a quarter century later, the battle still rages. Remember the premise of this chapter—you want Top Talent to choose your organization, and these incredibly talented people have options; they can work wherever they want. The war for these people will never end.

Don't make the mistake of sequestering the story with the Human Resources team. Yes, they can help, but a better idea is to deputize the entire organization. Think of this strategy as a literal force multiplier. How many employees do you have? If you are a nonprofit, how many donors do you have? Just imagine if all of these individuals could help Tell Your Story.

KPMG, a professional service company and one of the Big Four auditors, launched an initiative aimed at inspiring their workforce to reach new levels of engagement by reframing and elevating the meaning and purpose of their work. To achieve this goal, KPMG needed to first articulate a higher purpose. Extensive research and hundreds of interviews resulted in a new purpose statement: Inspire Confidence. Empower Change. KPMG recognized just telling people from the top down about their higher purpose would not succeed. Leaders encouraged everyone—from interns to the CEO—to share their own stories about how their work is making a difference.[11]

The company developed an application that enabled their employees to create and share digital posters. They called the project the 10,000 Stories Challenge. In June, the company asked 27,000 partners and employees to create their own posters as individuals or teams. Leadership offered an incentive of two extra paid days off at the end of the year if they met the 10,000 stories goal by Thanksgiving. Employees surpassed the goal before the Fourth of July.

Leadership continued to receive thousands of stories even after the extra days off were assured. Clearly, the incentive wasn't the primary motivator; employees simply wanted to express the meaning of their work. By Thanksgiving, leadership had received nearly 42,000 stories.[12]

By connecting employees to a Bigger Vision, morale scores soared, turnover plummeted, and the firm also enjoyed one of its best years in recent history. Ninety percent of partners reported the higher-purpose initiatives increased people's pride in KPMG. This improvement in morale also resulted in KPMG surging 17 spots on *Fortune* magazine's annual 100 Best Companies to Work For list. Later that year, KPMG was also ranked number one of the Big Four accounting firms in the United States for the first time in its history.[13]

Maybe you don't think you can get 42,000 stories from your associates, but there are things you can do. Here are a few ideas to help you better Tell the Story.

Align Your Message. Are you clear on what you have to offer Top Talent? Are you aligned on the messaging? If not, this should be job one. You cannot successfully cascade a message that lacks clarity.

If you want to assess your current status, it's really simple. At your next meeting, ask all the attendees—whether you have five or five hundred people in the room—a single question:

If someone asked you why they should consider working at our organization, what would you tell them?

Ask everyone to write down their answers and turn them in. The verbiage doesn't need to be precise. Just check to see how many include something about being well-led, personal growth, and the opportunity to be part of something bigger than themselves.

Leverage Social Media. Word of mouth and referrals will always be powerful, but what if you want to share your story with a broader audience? Social media may be your answer.

One Chick-fil-A restaurant we worked with in California decided to change the messaging on their Instagram account. They made the bold decision to no longer feature the food. On the surface, this struck us as strange. The leader's explanation provided the logic behind the counterintuitive decision.

The restaurant Operator told Randy, "Whoever visits our IG knows we have food. We are a restaurant. Now we have pictures to reflect our talent strategy. We feature stories about our employees and their leaders, stories about how our people are growing, and the impact we are making in the community. This shift has raised the quality of our applicants and improved our level of talent."

Train Everyone. We would suggest you do training sessions for your employees to help them understand what you are doing and why. They also need to understand the role you want them to play.

Don't overthink this. You could do a series of webinars, or Lunch 'n Learn sessions. Don't drop the ball here. Having a clear message with cool tools won't matter if your people don't embrace their role as ambassadors in search of Top Talent.

PRACTICE!

Create a plan to mobilize your entire workforce as ambassadors on a quest to recruit Top Talent. If you aren't personally creating the plan, determine who will be accountable, who will be on their team, what resources they will need, and when the effort will officially launch. You may want to go back to page 59 to find a refresher on creating a Team Charter.

GONE FISHIN'

The mind is a funny thing. Have you ever noticed how you can from time to time connect seemingly random things in a meaningful way? This phenomenon, often referred to as associative learning, happened to Mark while he and the team worked to discover what Top Talent wants in a job.

While he and the team were trying to make sense of the reams of research data, his father died. As he reflected on their life together, he was thankful for so many wonderful memories. As he flipped through one memory and then another, it happened. He began to think about their fishing trips. He remembered how his dad always caught more fish than he did. As a kid, he chalked this up to the fact that big people catch more fish than little people.

As he fast-forwarded the memories of those fishing trips, he recalled that, as a teenager, his dad still outfished him. He remembers some low level of frustration but nothing serious; he loved the time with his dad. As an adult, Mark's dad continued to catch more fish than he did. If he was honest, this bothered him a little more. *What's the deal?* he thought. Then it hit him.

Mark realized he had seen his dad fish with many different baits over the years. One day, he fished with crickets, and another day pink worms. The next outing he might be fishing with minnows. He had seen him use numerous artificial lures of varying types—crank bait, top water plugs, spinner baits, and more.

On the other hand, Mark loved to fish with plastic worms. It was easier: cleaner, no worm guts on your hands, and no need to change his setup. He would from time to time change to a different color rubber worm with little effect. Most days, Mark caught nothing because he wasn't fishing with the right bait. Mark's dad was always willing to change the bait to accommodate the desires of the fish.

What does any of this have to do with attracting Top Talent? Everything! Many organizations are fishing with rubber worms because it's what they like to fish with. It's simple. It's easy. It's clean, and requires little thought . . . even if the fish aren't biting. However, the smart angler and the smart organizations know what bait will work in different conditions.

Our team spent several years and millions of dollars talking to the fish (Top Talent). We know what they want: a Better Boss, a Brighter Future, and a Bigger Vision. We've had some leaders tell us they don't like this. Sorry. This is what Top Talent is biting on.

We talked to a senior leader in a multibillion-dollar organization after he read *Talent Magnet*. He said the content we shared was going to change everything. "How?" we asked. He said, "We've never considered what Top Talent wants in a job. We've always just offered what we offer." Sounds a lot like a rubber worm to us. You can occasionally catch a nice fish with this approach. Unfortunately, others, wisely regarding what the fish will bite, will out-fish you every time.

If you get this right, you're going to need a bigger boat.

MASTER TEAM BASICS

Mastering the basics is the first step to mastering the impossible.
—**Richard Branson**

Have you ever been on an extraordinary team? We hope you have. Unfortunately, most haven't. In the introduction to this section, we talked about the three levels of team performance: Underperformers, Good Teams, and High Performance Teams. According to research conducted by team experts and best-selling authors Jon Katzenbach and Douglas Smith, the odds of you being on a High Performance Team (our language, not theirs) is once in your lifetime.[1] We are going to help you crush those odds.

How can we make such a bold promise? Because we have trained thousands of teams in business, banking, education, not-for-profit, college and professional sports, law enforcement, health care, trade industries, and ministries around the world. Randy has even trained teams at the Internal Revenue Service. After more than two decades of helping build High Performance Teams, we can say with certainty that if you apply the practices in this chapter and the next, your probability of success will go from impossible to inevitable.

If this news is not enough to energize you, wait. There's more! The basic team skills you'll need on your high-performance journey are really simple—more than that, they are easy to learn and implement. Anyone of any age, educational level, vocation, or industry can put every one of the Team Basics to work starting today. The content in this chapter is essential to high performance and easy to understand and apply!

We're reading your mind again. At least some of you are confused. *If this content is so easy, accessible, and, did you say free . . . why are these ideas so foreign to most teams?*

One simple reason: lack of leadership. (This is also the answer to the question we posed at the beginning of this section: Why are most teams dysfunctional?) When something that exponentially improves performance is easy to learn and apply and is *free*, the only reasonable explanation for its absence is an absence of leadership. You can rectify this for your team!

TEAM PERFORMANCE CURVE

Not every group claiming to be a team is a team. You probably know this from experience. Following, you'll see a diagram that illustrates several ideas. We'll cover the various stages of a team's development and what elements are required to move up the curve.

Let's begin with the measure of a team's impact. Impact, or performance, is represented on the y-axis. We assume that every team has been assembled and charged to produce some kind of result. Therefore, whatever that is for your team can be measured on this axis.

The x-axis is the maturity of the team, not time. Often a long-standing group or team will assume they should be at the top of the curve. It doesn't work that way. Some teams can move up the curve quickly and others never advance. More on this in a moment.

TEAM PERFORMANCE CURVE

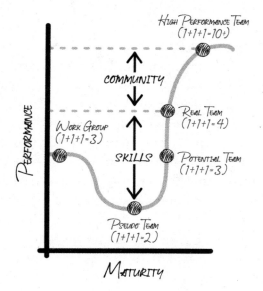

The starting point for many teams is as a Work Group. A Work Group is a collection of individuals who come together from time to time but work independently. Their performance is the sum of their individual efforts (1 + 1 + 1 = 3). Many Work Groups call themselves teams even though they are not.

You'll immediately notice the next stop on the curve is the Pseudo Team. Their defining attribute is that their performance is lower than a Work Group (1 + 1 + 1 = 2). How is this possible? Simply stated, they are an awful team. They would like to become a team and therefore they're investing the time and energy required to become a team, but they lack the critical skills, the Basics outlined in this chapter, to become a Real Team. This creates a mess.

When a team finds themselves here, they can retreat and go back up the curve to the safety of a Work Group. They abandon all this nonsense about becoming a team. Or, they get stuck and continue to frustrate people and waste resources (we've seen a lot of this over the years). Or, as we advocate, they move up the curve to the right. These dysfunctional teams do this by learning the Basics outlined in this chapter. The path forward is paved with the skills and disciplines we'll discuss on the following pages.

Along the way, as their skills grow, they reach a critical juncture. When their performance returns to their previous Work Group level, they are a Potential Team (1 + 1 + 1 = 3). Tragically, at this point, many turn back. Their reasoning can sound like this: "We only decided to become a team to improve performance and our performance is not any better than it was. Plus, we now have these meetings to schedule and Action Items to complete. It's a hassle without the reward. We're out."

What these teams lack in this moment is vision and leadership. They are so close to enjoying the fruit of their efforts . . . if they stay the course.

Assuming they do continue on their journey, the Team Basics and the skills they include will, over time, elevate the group's performance to Real Team status (1 + 1 + 1 = 4). This is an amazing and defining moment in the life of any team: the moment they realize they are producing more results working together than they could have working independently. What's next? Many teams stop at this point. They assume their quest is complete.

For many, their journey ends because they don't know there is another level of performance—a High Performance Team (1 + 1 + 1 = 10+). And even if they might speculate about its existence, few know the path forward. The Basic skills you're about to learn will not take you there. However, no team can scale the rest of the curve without them. The Basics are the launching pad for true greatness. This final leg of the journey is paved with Genuine Community, the topic for our next chapter.

Before we jump in to the Basics, take a long look at the performance curve. Where is your current team? What do you need to move forward? You have to start where you are but you don't have to stay there.

THE BASICS

Our temptation as we write this chapter is to try to cover too much. We have resisted. Yes, there are a few topics you could arguably add to our list of Basics that we've chosen to omit, but we wanted to only share those that create a foundation for future performance and those with the most short-term impact. Seven Basics will help any team move up the Team Performance Curve. Here we go!

#1 Create Role Clarity
Many of the problems we encounter in team-based organizations stem from a lack of role clarity. This was clearly illustrated when a leader approached Mark and shared his frustration with his leaders. The point leader wanted his team to solve problems and, by his account, they weren't. To make matters worse, this was not a new development. Here's how the conversation unfolded.

"My leaders just aren't solving problems," the leader lamented.

"Can you give me an example?" Mark asked.

"Sure. Yesterday, I walked in and found a huge issue. The team leader didn't even acknowledge the problem."

"So, what did you do?"

"I solved the problem," he said with a note of pride.

"You're good at solving problems, aren't you?"

"I am," he said as a broad smile broke across his face.

"And you enjoy doing it?"

"I do."

Mark decided to challenge his old friend. "Okay, based on this brief consulting intervention, I think you have a credibility problem with your team. You say you want them to solve problems but they don't believe you."

"Why not?"

"Because you always jump in and solve the problem. You really don't have role clarity on this issue. Here's my recommendation: The next time you encounter a problem your leaders have overlooked or failed to address, pull one of them aside and say something like this: 'We have two problems here: One, the issue at hand. Our second problem is the fact I'm having to point it out to you.'"

It's never your job to do their job. As the leader, you must be absolutely clear on who is accountable for what. If you've decided that you want your leaders to identify and solve problems, your role is to train and resource them to do so.

But how do you decide who should do what? It really depends on several factors: the structure you are trying to build, the skills of those around you, the urgency of an issue, and the long-term impact or implications of an issue, to name a few. Establishing role clarity is an ongoing process. As the team matures and the needs of the organization change, so can roles.

When Peter Drucker was asked, "What's the most important decision a leader makes?" he said, "Who does what." Ultimately, the point leader has to decide who will do what.

Assuming you want to build a High Performance Team, a team capable of managing the day-to-day operations, while improving performance, here's a good starting point:

Leader's Role	Team's Role
Provide vision	Communicate vision
Establish values	Enforce values
Establish core strategies	Identify and solve problems
Provide resources	Lift and maintain engagement
Provide encouragement	Train and equip team members
Develop senior leaders	Develop next-generation leaders
Establish boundaries	Provide accountability
Clarify roles	Improve performance

If you want your teams to excel, be sure there is no question regarding who does what. You may be shocked by the value this simple exercise will create within your team and organization.

One of our clients owns a plumbing company. Randy recalls the owner's breakthrough moment.

"I decided to unload my truck."

"You did what?" Randy asked.

The owner explained how he was working for his company but not leading it. He had two technicians who were on jobsites every day just like he was, and his wife was taking calls and collecting the bills. He said, "I knew we would never grow to our full potential without a leader. So, I went home one evening, unloaded my tools, and put them in the garage. I packed a small tool bag for emergencies and drove our car to the office the next day. I started building our business. I haven't looked back."

This leader cites this incident as the defining moment for his organization. He had new levels of role clarity. With the truck parked in the garage and tools stowed away, he was able to grow from a staff of four, including his wife, to more than 50 employees. By his own account, the leader said "the unlock" for their growth was a single, role-clarifying decision.

Is it possible you need to "unload your truck" to build your organization?

> **Role clarity is one of the most powerful tools in your leadership toolbox.**

PRACTICE!

Refer to our sample roles list; now draft your own version. Then, sit with your leaders to determine what, if any, changes need to be made. Once you are clear on roles, you can shift your focus to preparing individuals and the team with the skills they will need to be successful.

#2 Establish Team Purpose

We talked at length earlier about the importance of vision for an organization. Team purpose is another form of vision. Have you ever been on a team that didn't know why it existed? We hope not. Believe us, it's not fun. Every team deserves to know why they exist. Have you had this conversation? Is everyone on the same page? A tried-and-true technique we have used and recommended for years is to simply ask folks in your next meeting to write down their answer to the following question: Why does our team exist? Be sure they write their answers on something they can hand in. We like 3 x 5 notecards. Read the responses out loud, allowing no commentary, explanation, or defense. If everyone has the same answer, congratulations. Our guess is many of you will need to work on this. If this is your situation, don't beat yourself up—fix it.

Mark had the opportunity to consult with a storied organization. They were established over 100 years ago. During a meeting with their senior leaders, he had an uncomfortable feeling the group was not aligned on much of anything including why the senior team existed. Rather than sharing his concern directly, he used the 3 x 5 card trick, and asked everyone to answer one question: *Why does this organization exist?* He knew it would be futile to tackle the team problem without at least noting the bigger issue.

His instincts were correct. When he read the cards aloud for the group, it was notable that there were 12 very well-articulated and totally different responses.

Perhaps this is clear, but we don't want you to miss it: The reason teams outperform individuals is due to the constructive collaboration that exists when you have a group of people pursuing a *common* goal or objective. The promise and potential of synergy is unattainable if the individuals are pursuing different goals. Here's a real-world example from Mark's son's high school basketball team.

Justin's team was fortunate to have some extremely gifted players. One would go on to play in the NBA. Seeing Pat Riley and Jerry West in the stands for a game or having Division I coaches attend practices was really fun. The problem with the team was their lack of a shared purpose. Obviously, our NBA-bound player had his own priorities, while others were looking to pad their stats and impress college coaches. Still others really just wanted to have a good time. Some actually wanted to win games. Yes, the team won some games, but they should have won them all. Lack of a unifying purpose virtually guarantees suboptimized performance. And don't assume some self-centered or nefarious intent. If leaders don't establish the why, the team will rarely figure it out on their own, even if the desired outcome seems obvious to the casual observer.

Why does your team exist? Here are a few of the responses we've encountered in the past:

- Grow people and grow the business.
- Execute the plan.
- Grow the organization's leadership capacity.
- Create a fun place to work.

Your odds of creating a High Performance Team increase exponentially if you and your team are clear on why they exist. Don't make them guess.

┌ **PRACTICE!** ─────────

If you haven't already, establish the purpose of your team (and if you are the senior leader, you may want to begin this process for every team you have in your organization). If you believe your purpose is already clear, ask your team to be sure.

#3 Set Team Goals

The power of goals is well documented. Therefore, we'll not talk about why you should have goals other than to say well-conceived and thoughtful goals improve performance. Here are a few tips to help you set better goals.

Look at your past performance. What can you learn from your historical performance? How much untapped potential do you believe you have as a team? Are you on an uptrend or in a downward trajectory?

Look at the context. Do you see any events, obstacles, opportunities, or circumstances that will likely impact your performance in the coming months or years? These can be positive or negative (e.g., a major competitor shutting down could boost sales, or closing one of your locations for remodeling could depress sales).

Ask the team for input. When invited to the table, it's amazing how often teams will set higher goals than leadership would. Mark recalls a story from a nonprofit organization he served. The team he was leading set a goal to double their historical average attendance for an upcoming event. It was a far more aggressive goal than he would have set. After sensing the team's energy and excitement, he supported the goal. In the end, the team achieved about 90% of their audacious goal. This was still far beyond their normal output. This example reminds us to, whenever appropriate, solicit team input before establishing the final goal(s) for the team.

Be sure your goals stretch the team. There is research to support the idea that goals that drive the most performance are neither too hard nor too easy. If the team perceives the goal as too hard, they will not offer their best effort. If they think the goal is too easy, they may feel it doesn't require their best effort. Our recommendation is to set a goal with a 50% probability of success. This will drive maximum effort and contribution.

PRACTICE!

Establish three to five team goals using the guidelines above. You can do this unilaterally or involve the team as you see fit. Our general counsel is to make this a consultative decision with the leader retaining the final call. We'll talk more about your decision-making options later in this chapter.

#4 Build Your Scorecard

A scorecard is critical for monitoring the ongoing performance of your team. What are the key health indicators your team is charged with improving? If key health indicators is a new term for you, think about a visit to your primary care physician or even the emergency room. One of Randy's daughters is a physician's assistant. If you visit her office, regardless of your ailment, she will start by checking your "vitals." Typically, these are pulse, blood pressure, and temperature. These are your key health indicators. Then, she'll check on whatever sent you to the doctor's office in the first place.

Your team scorecard may reflect a direct measure of your ultimate goals, or it may contain project-based metrics, or both. Many businesses have a core set of metrics that never change (e.g., sales and profits), while others do change with the needs of the business. There may be a push to find 100,000 new customers over the next 12 months or a challenge to reduce turnover by 25% over the next year. These are targets that would probably warrant a spot on the scorecard, at least for the term of the project. The best scorecards are dynamic—they are a tool to serve the team or organization.

We have found the most helpful scorecards provide focus for the team. Therefore, you don't want too many things to track. How many? Just like our previous recommendation about goals, fewer is better. A good starting point would be three to seven.

During a visit with a senior leader from Southwest Airlines, he shared a breakthrough they'd had about measurement. Known for being a data-driven company, they once had 44 key metrics on their scorecard. It was a staggering number—practically overwhelming—and their team soon realized they needed to narrow their focus. While they admitted they would continue tracking many numbers, they decided to concentrate on just eight.

We congratulated him on the improvement, but couldn't help

pointing out that eight, though a significant reduction from 44, still seemed like quite a lot. Our host paused for a moment, then smiled. "You caught me," he said. "We really have three primary metrics—with five supporting numbers."

You can track as many key numbers as you would like. We recommend separating them into two groups, which we call page one and page two metrics. Page one contains numbers you look at all the time. Page two numbers can serve as secondary diagnostics if the numbers on page one are out of whack.

Here are a few ideas on how to use your scorecard.

Use the data as an early warning system. Because you're using the scorecard to track performance over time, you can spot unhealthy trends early. Once you spot a trend line you want to change, you'll create some type of intervention to change the trajectory of the trend.

Track the impact of interventions. It's fun to draw an intervention line on a performance graph and see what happens. If the line turns in a positive direction, it's good news and your intervention was a success—congratulations! If the line stays the same or goes in the wrong direction, congratulations! You know you need to try something else.

Your scorecard should signal when it's time to celebrate. Most teams don't celebrate enough. Some celebrate without due cause. This disingenuous display of accomplishment doesn't really help. You could even unintentionally undermine your leadership and earn the label of being out of touch. Legitimate celebration triggered by hitting performance milestones is only possible if you are tracking your performance over time.

┌─ **PRACTICE!** ──────────────────────────────┐

Create the first draft of your team scorecard. You can do
this alone or with input from the team. If you create it on
your own, we recommend asking the team to help you
improve on the work you've done.

└──┘

#5 Conduct Great Meetings

Some of you may be wondering why meetings would be included
on a list of Team Basics. It's simple: The best teams have the best
meetings. If you want to know if a teacher can teach, you watch
them in the classroom. If you want to know the prowess of a
swimmer, observe them in the pool. If you want an insight into
the capability of a leader, watch them run a meeting.

Just like chipping and putting determine the level of success a
golfer enjoys, meetings are a leader's short game. The vision talks
can be impressive, like a 300-yard tee shot. But if the golfer can't
score, they lose. The same is true for leaders. The vision will only
take you so far. Can you get the ball in the hole?

Many leaders have convinced themselves that meetings are a
waste. Unfortunately, this has become a self-fulfilling prophecy.
The low expectations have translated into even lower standards.
The result: Most meetings *are* terrible. According to one study
from Atlassian, 72% of meetings are ineffective![2] However, this
finding is not the format's fault. Meetings are a tool. In the hands
of a talented and skilled leader, meetings can be extraordinary.

Think about what you can do in a well-conceived and well-
executed team meeting:

- Cast vision
- Establish priorities
- Reinforce priorities
- Set goals
- Resolve conflict
- Solve problems

- Build community
- Facilitate development
- Allocate resources
- Create plans
- Give the gift of accountability

- Unite people
- Celebrate success
- Strengthen culture
- Cascade key messages
- Call out the best in people

Meetings that do these things add *huge* value. We're not sure how you can look at the list above and say meetings are a waste of time unless your meetings don't include these elements.

Notice what is not on the list—updates and complaints. This is what far too many meetings have been allowed to degenerate into. There are more efficient ways to update your team on what's going on. Information sharing should be kept to a bare minimum. And while complaints should be acknowledged, the best leaders capture and prioritize them to discern how to move to the solution side of the issue—often outside the meeting.

What if we told you the time you invest in meetings could be the most profitable hours on your calendar? Here's how to do it. (You can thank us later.)

Appoint a facilitator. A facilitator's role is to anticipate and remove barriers before, during, and after the meeting. Be sure someone is assigned to play this critical role.

Prepare an agenda. In order to prepare an effective agenda, the facilitator must prioritize the topics to be discussed, determine the desired outcome for each item, decide who should lead each segment, figure out which topics require pre-work, and decide how much time to allocate to each item.

Distribute the agenda in advance. Some members of the team will never be able to contribute fully without advance time to prepare. Help them, and the team, by sending out the agenda in advance. You may need to survey your team members to determine how much prep time people need. Don't be surprised if some want the agenda several days before the meeting.

Invite the right people. Have you ever been frustrated when you were in a meeting and realized you were missing an important perspective? Maybe you didn't even have the decision-maker in the room. Always ask yourself, beforehand, "Who needs to be in this meeting?"

Distribute pertinent information in advance. Don't expect people to be handed vital information in the moment and offer substantive feedback. If there's something that needs to be reviewed or approved during the meeting, send it in advance whenever possible.

Show your work. Use a flip chart, or online tools for virtual meetings, to display your work. If you do, you'll find this practice aids with the creative process, enables the group to stay on task, and helps you reach productive conclusions on the items you discuss.

Focus on performance management. This is one of the meeting disciplines that has the potential to transform your team. A good rule of thumb is to invest 75% of the agenda on performance management. Performance management activities include: scorecard review, Action Item review, problem-solving, and recognition. The balance of the meeting can be devoted to community building, team development, and information sharing.

Include community building. Community turbocharges team

performance. If you remember the Team Performance Curve we described earlier, community is the multiplier and the differentiator between Good Teams and High Performance ones. You will not drift to deep levels of Genuine Community—you must invest the time. More on this in the next chapter.

Frame every agenda item. If you were in a meeting with us, you would notice we usually give the facilitator about 90 seconds to frame an agenda item before we raise the question, "*Why are we talking about this, and what is our desired outcome?*"

Keep the team focused. Stay on track. Many teams use a "parking lot" to record off-agenda topics that emerge during the meeting. You can decide later what to do with these items. Don't chase rabbits—they're really fast. You leave exhausted, with nothing to show for your effort.

Finish every Action Item. This doesn't mean you'll literally complete every item. It does mean everyone should know what next steps will be taken on each item. Some items will be taken outside the meeting for resolution; others may be moved to a future meeting. There may even be issues so time-sensitive you extend the time originally slotted for the item on your current agenda. Only when one of these decisions is made is the item finished.

Capture all Action Items. We covered this topic previously in the chapter on clarity but we couldn't leave it off our list of Team Basics. For some teams, this practice will be life-changing. Don't *just* talk about things. At the conclusion of *every* topic/agenda item, decide *who* will do *what* by *when*—and write it down.

Review previous Action Items. If you cultivate the discipline of reviewing the previous meeting's Action Items at *every* meeting, people will actually do what they've said they would do. Don't be afraid to give people the gift of accountability.

As you look at the items above, you may be wondering, *Do we have to do all of this?* You don't *have* to do any of it. But make no mistake, the more of these items you do, the better your meetings; the better your meetings, the better your team; and the better your team, the better your performance.

┌─ PRACTICE! ──────────────────────────

Use the items on the previous pages as a checklist for your upcoming meetings. Over time, see how many of these meeting-enhancing techniques you can incorporate.

#6 Solve Problems Together

A team is at their best when they are solving problems. Why are teams so good at solving problems? If you've built your team carefully, you have diverse opinions, disciplines, educational backgrounds, strengths, passions, and personalities. The combination of these multiple perspectives makes the *we* much smarter than the *me*. The team's collective IQ and problem-solving potential is astronomical! It's sad to think about how many teams are missing the moment. They are literally starving while sitting on a sandwich.

Why don't more teams engage in problem-solving on a regular basis? We think there are three primary reasons.

Problem-solving is time-consuming. Yes, this is true. However, the team should not entertain the easy problems. If a problem can be solved quickly, don't bother the team with it in the first place. Delegate the problem to a qualified leader—she can solve these problems without involving the team. For the more complex problems, you will need more time. In order to combat the time crunch, break your problem up and work on it over several meetings. If the situation is urgent, carve out the time before your next scheduled meeting.

Teams are squandering the time they do have on lower-value activities. Your meeting time is precious. You have the collective wisdom of your team together for a limited amount of time. How are you stewarding this resource? If you are spending your time merely catching up or sharing what's happening in your area, the opportunity cost is tremendous.

Teams haven't learned the skills of problem-solving. Obviously, this is not universally true, but we see this frequently. Mark recently talked to a veteran leader who wanted counsel on how to help his team learn to solve problems. The leader admitted they didn't know how to help them.

Mark told him the solution was simple: Select an appropriate problem-solving model and teach the team to use it. There are scores of models out there. Experiment. What you'll discover is that different models are best suited for different types of problems. Think of a problem-solving model like railroad tracks. Your team's brainpower is the locomotive. Without the tracks to run on, all the power resident in the engine is irrelevant.

We'll give you two models to get you started, one for system or process problems and another for issues involving an individual.

For system or process problems (e.g., defects, turnover, waste, declining sales), try a five-step approach:

1. **Define the Problem.** Pinpoint the problem as much as possible. One of our favorite quotes is "A problem well-defined is half-solved."

2. **Identify Potential Root Causes.** There are often numerous potential root causes. You must decide the one you want to solve for. If sales are down, do you think the primary root cause is inferior quality, a new low-cost competitor, or the fact you are operating without 25% of your staff, resulting in slow service? As you can imagine, a brainstorming session would be vastly different depending on which of these you decide to solve for. If you really do have multiple root causes, solve them separately, each with their own brainstorming and planning steps.

3. **Brainstorm Potential Solutions.** This is where many people start their problem-solving. Don't do this. Remember, you are brainstorming to address the single root cause the team identified.

4. **Create a Plan of Action.** Select your best idea(s) from the list you brainstormed, the ones you believe have the highest probability of addressing your problem. Then decide who will do what by when.

5. **Monitor Results.** Often, you won't know if your solution was successful for several weeks or months depending on the nature of your problem. If it was not successful, revisit each of the steps above. You may not have selected the right root cause to solve for, you may not have selected an adequate solution from your brainstormed options, or you may not have executed your plan successfully.

For a people problem, consider the ESRC model:[3]

- Does the person clearly understand what is *Expected* of them?
- Does the person have the necessary *Skills* to execute on the expectations?
- Does the person have the required *Resources* to meet the expectations?
- Does the person fully understand the *Consequences* of not meeting the expectations?

Look for an opportunity in the next week to try both of the approaches mentioned above.

Here's a quick warning: Problem-solving is as much an art as a science. Sometimes the process will yield spectacular results and other times your best efforts will fall short. We can recall many times when the solutions we championed didn't solve the problem we were addressing. The root cause of these failed interventions varies. Sometimes, you didn't pinpoint the problem adequately or you misidentified the root cause; therefore, your solution missed the mark. Maybe your solutions were flawed. Or, the plan the team created may not have been executed well. Our least favorite reason for a problem-solving effort that did not work is us—when the leader cannot move past their bias and preconceived answers. All of these causes are possible. When you stumble, don't be discouraged. If you are addressing real, significant, and often complex problems, their solutions can be elusive. Trust the process and do not give up!

```
┌─ PRACTICE! ─────────────────────────────────┐
```

PRACTICE!

Identify your biggest problem—the one that is having the greatest impact on your performance. Once again, you can decide this on your own or ask your team for input. After the problem has been identified, begin working through the appropriate problem-solving model. Don't be alarmed or discouraged if your efforts span more than one meeting. If you are addressing a huge problem, significant effort will likely be required to solve it.

#7 Improve Decision-Making

There is so much misinformation and even more confusion regarding decision-making in a team environment that we knew we had to include this critical topic in our list of Team Basics. Many say team decision-making is way too slow. It can be, but it doesn't have to be. Any time a decision needs to be made, the leader has four primary options.

Type One: Command Decision—In this case, the leader makes the decision. The team's role is to take good notes and ask clarifying questions about how to execute the leader's decision.

Type Two: Consultative Decision—For this type of decision, the leader invites input from others but makes the final decision.

Type Three: Consensus Decision—These are decisions that are reached by the team. True consensus decisions are ones requiring the group to reach a decision that everyone in the group can *fully* support. Consensus decisions, by definition, are never the product of a vote. Consensus is the most time-consuming type of decision-making—use it sparingly.

Type Four: Delegated Decision—This is when the leader gives the decision to someone else—usually an individual, but sometimes the team.

A cautionary note: Leaders must be honest in the use of these options. We've seen this scenario—a leader came to a team and said, "We have a decision to make and I'd like it to be consultative." However, after some discussion, a team member called out the leader and said, "It sounds like you've already made a decision and you don't want to tell us. If this is really a command decision, own it. Don't try to get our buy-in by faking a consultative decision."

The leader responded, "I haven't decided yet. What you're hearing is my personal bias. I do have an opinion. That's why I'm seeking your counsel—to help me evaluate and challenge my current thinking." Now that's a good decision-making process and wonderful team behavior!

As crazy as this may sound, this simple framework really works. If you'll take five minutes and share these four decision types with your team, your decision-making process will improve, you'll save time, and you'll make better decisions.

PRACTICE!

Invest 5 minutes at your next team meeting to teach everyone the four types of decision-making and begin using this approach immediately.

Now that you understand the Team Basics, you're ready to approach the summit of the Team Performance Curve. High Performance is within your reach! Getting to the next level of performance will require two things. First, a leap of faith. What we're about to explore in the next chapter is not only the final piece to the puzzle you may have been trying to solve your entire career; the concept will be foreign to most leaders. Trust us, we've done this many times over the years with breathtaking results.

Beyond faith, you'll need only one indispensable ingredient: leadership. Your team will not march up the performance curve on their own. In the absence of leadership, the vast majority of teams either get stuck or retreat to the mediocrity and comfort of their Work Group. No team drifts to high performance. You will be the one to provide the focus and energy required to take new ground. We're thankful your team has you to show them the way.

BUILD GENUINE COMMUNITY

For the strength of the pack is the wolf, and the strength of the wolf is the pack.
—**Rudyard Kipling**

The year was 480 BC. The Persian King Xerxes was a man on a mission. He was living in the past, the present, and the future. He was on a march to avenge his father's defeat at the Battle of Marathon a decade earlier. His plan was to engage the Greeks by land and sea. The king wanted to secure a land route to the heartland of Greece, break their spirit, and reduce their resistance to his impending invasion. Ultimately, he wanted to expand his empire by capturing Greece. He also wanted to surpass his father's conquests and fortify his status as a legendary conqueror. Needless to say, there was a lot going on in the head and the heart of the king. All of his grand plans hinged on moving his massive army through a small pass at Thermopylae.[1]

As it turned out, this would be no easy task. Defending the pass were King Leonidas and his Palace Guard—the 300 finest warriors Greece had to offer. They were joined by a small number of allies. What made this battle so interesting was the audacity and tenacity of the Greeks. When it was reported that the Persian archers would fire so many arrows they would block out the sun, the historian Herodotus reports the Spartan response was, "Good, we shall fight in the shade."[2]

What gave the Spartans so much confidence? The complete answer to that question is far beyond the scope of this work, but at the heart of Leonidas's confidence was a lifetime of preparation combined with a deep sense of unity and commitment among his men.

One physical manifestation of the disciplined training and their ultimate trust in each other was a military move called the phalanx. The Spartans were renowned for their mastery of this technique.[3]

The tactic itself was comprised of a densely packed rectangular formation in which each man's shield overlapped with the next. The men stood shoulder to shoulder. Success in execution depended on discipline and coordinated movements. Every man was counting on his fellow man to provide his defense. The phalanx was so effective, it became feared by their enemies.

This and other examples from the Greeks make us believe the Spartans understood the concept of community. When you combine this ethos of communal effort and mutual support with the skills they spent their lives developing, it's easy to see why the Spartans were such a formidable force.

Many of you may know how the story of the 300 ended. Here's what author and historian Steven Pressfield wrote in *Gates of Fire*: "King Xerxes and his troops did overtake Leonidas and his personal guard of 300 elite soldiers—it only took two million Persian soldiers to do so."[4]

What could your team accomplish, against all odds, and, unlike the Spartans, live to tell about it? The only way to find out is to build Genuine Community.

THAT ODD THING YOU DO

Many years ago, Mark and his team embarked on a mission to determine why most teams flounder and so very few flourish. We've already foreshadowed what they learned when we introduced the Team Performance Curve. The short answer is that High Performance Teams are an amalgamation of two distinct ingredients: Team Basics—the skills, practices, and disciplines outlined in the previous chapter—and community, the subject of this chapter.

When Mark began this work to discover why some teams significantly outperformed others, he and his team really didn't know what they were looking for. However, they were sold on the power of teams. They knew teams consistently outperform individuals working alone or independently (see our previous comments regarding Work Groups on page 123). Armed with this steadfast belief in the power and potential of teams, Mark and his team started the organization's team training. This was in the days before they stumbled on the idea of community. Therefore, the training and consulting firm they hired were experts in "team management." Looking back, their agenda focused exclusively on the Basics we covered in the previous chapter. This was a very productive season for the organization and they built a number of Real Teams (1 + 1 + 1 = 4).

During one of the coaching sessions in which the consultant actually sat in a meeting with the team to provide "process feedback," she offered an observation. "I really don't know what to make of that odd thing you do at the beginning of your meeting. However, it seems to be helping, so I would suggest you keep doing it."

The "odd thing" was the first item on the team's agenda at every meeting. Today, we would call it community building, although they didn't have a name for it at the time. The team had just intuitively added it to the agenda. Each team member was given the opportunity to give a brief personal update. Because many of the team members had worked together for a long time, some of the updates were very personal in nature.

Early in their team journey, they discovered that every team has two agendas: a task agenda covering the outcomes you are charged with producing and a social agenda focused on the team's people and their lives at work and beyond. Most teams we've encountered over the years focus only on the task agenda. The team was searching for a way to honor this shadow, or secondary, agenda. So, they added time at the beginning of every meeting to catch up. Little did he know what they were tinkering with was the real power behind the performance of the team. For years, they continued to experiment and search, always looking for ways to enhance the performance of their teams.

Their moment of clarity came while reading a book by two thought leaders in the field of team dynamics, Jon R. Katzenbach and Douglas K. Smith. In *The Wisdom of Teams*, they describe a rare team, one capable of extraordinary levels of performance— performance far beyond reasonable norms. They said this output was the result of deep levels of care for each other as well as the work. However, they described this level of care as a fluke.[5] They went as far as saying you can expect this type of team to form, on average, only once in a career. Think of something akin to spontaneous combustion; if the conditions are exactly right, it might happen, but most of us have never witnessed it in real life.

From this point forward, Mark and the team began to actively seek ways to cultivate the level of care and concern that Katzenbach and Smith described while at the same time they worked to master the Team Basics we discussed in the last chapter. The new idea for them was that they could intentionally and strategically create what Katzenbach and Smith saw as a grand cosmic accident. They called it *community*.

WHAT IS COMMUNITY?

Community is a place, an incredibly special place. Community is where you are honored, respected, and valued as a human being. It is a place where people can find safety while taking risks. This is no ordinary space—here, you can push and prod and challenge your colleagues to think deeper and work harder. This is a place where people care deeply about the work and those they work with. Community is a place that's hard to describe because it is so rare; there are few places like it on the planet. Most adults have never experienced it at the level we are striving to create. Community is a feeling. It is emotional, transformational, and enduring in mind and spirit, if not in practice. Once you have experienced it, if you lose it, you'll work desperately to re-create it. Finally,

Community is a multiplier for team performance.

While all of the above is true, we found our attempts to define community continued to fall short of the reality. The more we talked and wrote, the more we rambled, searching for the ever-elusive, perfect language. If you want to feel our struggle, try to define *love* for someone who hasn't experienced it. To end the madness, we adopted a simple three-part, action-based definition.

Armed with a clear and actionable definition, *community* becomes more than a concept—now, you can pursue it strategically. The balance of this chapter will provide a deeper look at the three elements of Genuine Community. Community is a place where you: Know Deeply, Serve Willingly, and Do Life Together.

KNOW DEEPLY

The cornerstone of community is to know and be known. How much do you know about those on your team? There is a psychological and emotional bond that forms when people really know each other. That bond is like a deepening well; the more you know, the deeper the bond. Therefore, community is cumulative—it grows with each bit of information and shared experience. Over months, years, and, if you're fortunate, decades, the well grows so deep, you don't know where it ends.

We constantly engage with teams who are virtually strangers. We've asked team members to introduce themselves and tell us something about their lives, only to be interrupted by others from the team. "I never knew that."

When probing the power of knowing another human deeply and its impact on the team, someone once said, "It's hard to give up on someone once you know their story." Do you know the story of the members of your team? Not just the old-timers and those who've been with you for years. What about the new people?

We once had a leader tell us his team was no longer clicking. The conversation was hysterical. When asked what had changed, he said, "Nothing." The follow-up question was, "Was the team 'clicking' in the past?"

"Yes," he insisted.

"So, something must have changed."

"No, nothing has changed." He was adamant.

After an extended exchange, the leader admitted he had several new members on his team.

"That's it!" we said. "You've just invited a couple of strangers to sit around your kitchen table with your long-standing team members. They don't know each other."

Knowing others deeply and personally is foundational to community, and it is where you must begin your journey.

Invest the Time

Time on task is required to build Genuine Community. When Mark talked with Jon Katzenbach about his team's thoughts and experiences, Jon believed we had discovered an insight—community could probably be created strategically, he admitted. He also suggested that community could be forged by accident in the crucible of extreme circumstances. He explained that if folks survive a plane crash, the shared traumatic experience will create a sense of community immediately.

Mark said, "Yes, I guess it would, but people die in plane crashes. We're going to help people build community without anyone dying. Granted, it will take a little longer, but we like the process much better."

The following are activities you can begin immediately to build community.

Allocate Meeting Time. Team meetings are a prime opportunity for community building—if you, as the leader, put community building time on the agenda and are validating its importance and priority for the team. Community is not optional or extracurricular; it must be part of your core performance strategy. When you allocate precious time to this in your meetings, it communicates volumes.

How much time? This is a bit tricky. It depends. If you have a new team member, you may over-index on community-building time in a meeting. You are trying to inculcate this new person as quickly as possible. You may even schedule something outside the meeting for the sole purpose of helping the new person acclimate and join your community. If you are in a business-as-usual mode, we refer you back to the ideal meeting structure. Seventy-five percent of your time together should be focused on performance management. The remaining 25% can be divided as needed among community building, team development, and information sharing.

Tell Your Story. A terrific way to begin the Know Deeply phase of the process is to ask everyone to tell their story. Depending on the size of your team and the context (e.g., a normal team meeting, onboarding for a new team member, a retreat setting), you'll need to decide how much time to allocate and this will determine how many people can share their story in a given meeting. You may want to do this at every meeting for a few months until everyone has had their turn. One cautionary note: Don't shortchange this! Don't say, "You've got three minutes to tell your story." You be the judge, but we would recommend you give everyone at least 10 minutes (15 would be better).

If you're feeling creative and have the time to allocate, here's an idea that can be revealing and facilitate the process of helping everyone tell their story. We did this activity at a team retreat so time was not a significant concern. We asked every team member to bring eight to ten pocket-sized objects that reflect a facet of their life story. Once everyone arrived, we handed them a transparent box (we believe they were originally designed to display basketballs). We asked everyone to build a display using the artifacts they had brought with them. We also provided craft supplies for mounting and displaying their work. We gave everyone a couple of hours to build their "You Cube" and prepare their remarks. Each person would have time the next day to present their finished cube and tell their story. When we returned to the office, we displayed all the cubes in the entryway to our team's office area.

Explore the Ordinary. Some of you have been part of meetings that began with what the host/facilitator might have called an "icebreaker." These can be fun. They can also be purposeful. What if you commandeered the first few minutes of a meeting to go a little deeper to build community? Why not ask questions to help the group know each person better? These questions don't have to be deep or philosophical; it's probably better if they aren't. Remember, community is cumulative and builds over time. Every data point that helps you know your teammates better is a good thing. Here are a few questions to stimulate your creativity:

- What is your favorite color?
- What is your favorite food?
- What's your favorite movie?
- What's your favorite childhood memory?
- What was your favorite class in high school?
- Where did you grow up?
- If you could live anywhere in the world, where would you live?
- What would you do if you won the lottery?
- If you could have any superpower, what would you choose?

As the team begins to know more and more of these seemingly trivial things about each other, you can gradually increase the challenge level of the questions. Don't move too quickly to this next level—depending on how much time you spend together, you should think in terms of months, not weeks. Examples of these deeper questions include:

- If you could turn back the clock, what would you do differently?
- What worries you most about the future?
- What scares you?
- What keeps you up at night?
- If you were going to change professions, what would you do?
- Who is your hero?
- What do you want to be true in your personal life in a year that's not true today?
- What do you want your legacy to be?

You can see why you don't want to ask questions like these until you've built adequate levels of trust.

PRACTICE!

Go back and look at the agendas from your last five team meetings. How much time, if any, was devoted to building community? Going forward, *always* include some time on the agenda for this crucial performance-enhancing activity.

SERVE WILLINGLY

We have a special place in our lives for people who serve us willingly. Think about someone you have a deep personal relationship with. Our guess is you are willing to serve them. And when you think about the people who have served you over your life and career, what emotions come to mind? Gratitude? Loyalty? Appreciation?

Coach Lou Holtz, most famously remembered for his National Championship at the University of Notre Dame, was a huge fan of community building as a performance-enhancing strategy, although he didn't call it community. We believe he would have described his understanding of this illusive and mysterious element required for elite levels of team performance as a progressive revelation over his coaching career. His insights on this topic were grounded in tactical and behavioral activities he controlled as the leader. He realized he could do things to foster deep and personal relationships among his players. The better he did this, the more their performance improved.

One strategy he learned to value was the power of serving. Coach Holtz told Mark that he ended every practice by calling the team together and asking them how they could serve each other. He said the answers varied widely, from "I need a ride" to "I have a math test tomorrow—can someone help me study tonight?" The coach said his response to the math request was, "Does anyone here know how to do math?" The team laughed, and they found someone to serve the player in need.

It's hard to overstate the camaraderie and commitment you can cultivate in a place where serving and allowing yourself to be served is the norm. Try it—you'll like what you discover. The following are several tips to make serving second nature.

Be Intentional

If you think about it, many of the best things in life require some intentionality. Lifelong friendships don't nurture themselves. An adequate retirement nest egg didn't mysteriously appear in your bank account. Generally, health and fitness are the outcome of our intentional lifestyle choices. To enjoy a long and rewarding career requires some forethought. A college education or a new hobby both demand some premeditated actions. This list could become insanely long very quickly. Here's a blinding flash of the obvious: You'll serve more if you are intentional.

Be Proactive

As the Holtz story above illustrates, he initiated the end-of-practice huddle as an opportunity to probe for opportunities to serve. If he hadn't asked, we're not sure the player would have sought out the help he needed as he prepped for his upcoming test. What would happen if you and your team included the question "How can we serve one another?" every time you met?

You can also make this part of your approach as a leader outside your team meetings. How often do you ask a member of your team, "How can I serve you?" Now, the disclaimer here is that you do have to be careful; some people will see this as an open door to delegate up. To avoid this pitfall, we recommend reading the book *The One Minute Manager Meets the Monkey*. The book's premise is that problems, issues, and sometimes ongoing responsibilities are a lot like monkeys who require care and feeding. Ken Blanchard and his coauthors offer the cautionary note to not let other people's monkeys jump on your back. If they do, you are now responsible for their care and feeding. Don't let this prevent you from looking for opportunities to serve—just be aware.

You should always be on the lookout for legitimate and appropriate opportunities to serve those on your team. People always watch the leader. Your example will set the standard for others.

Do the Unexpected

Helping someone with a PowerPoint presentation is a good thing to do. Showing a new employee how to submit an expense report counts as serving too. Don't minimize the mundane, but also think bigger and bolder. What would be unexpected help?

We recently heard a story from decades ago, and the individual we met is still talking about it. He had just accepted a new job. He and his family would be moving to the town where the company was headquartered. On moving day, with the truck in the yard and boxes being shuffled into empty rooms, he looked up and his new boss was there. He was shocked, and before he could inquire about why he was there, the man said, "I just came to help." Imagine the impact this encounter had on this man and his family. He hadn't even started yet and the person he would be reporting to, his team leader, was standing in his driveway wanting to serve him and his family.

One more story. We know a team leader who learned that a member of his team wanted to adopt a baby. He knew enough to know the process is often exhausting, full of emotions, and can extend for months and years. In a conversation with the employee about the process, he learned they hadn't officially begun. When he asked when they would begin, he was told they didn't have the money to formally start the process. The leader wrote a personal check so they could begin the process that culminated in a baby girl joining their family.

What could you do to serve members of your team such that they will still be talking about it decades later?

PRACTICE!

Find some way to serve a member of your team this week. If you are willing to share what you did, we would love to hear from you. Any other details about your experience would be appreciated. As always, we want to cheer you on. Send your story to **Info@LeadEveryDay.com**.

DO LIFE TOGETHER

Have you ever thought seriously about what makes plants grow? Neither of us are gardeners but we know you need good soil, the right amount of sunshine and water, good seed, and the proper nutrients. All of these things combined will drastically increase your probability of success. What are the elements required to help you cultivate authentic community? We've covered several of them here. What we've not addressed is the mindset you need to develop.

Your goal, if you want to build Genuine Community, is to enter the life of your teammates and invite them to enter yours. You need to be there for the highs and the lows, the setbacks, the successes, the hopes, dreams, fears, uncertainties, wins and losses, the tragedies and the triumphs. You need to Do Life Together.

Escape Your Comfort Zone

Doing life together is not always comfortable. As we've mentioned above, there will be good times and challenging ones—weddings and funerals. From time to time, you'll have to break the routines of the work and just be present with people. For many leaders, paying attention to the needs of others will always require our focused attention. We'll also have to learn to embrace the discomfort. The best leaders are comfortable being uncomfortable. Think about the best leaders you've ever known; our bet is they had the ability to resist comfort and move boldly toward the people they were attempting to lead. The good news is the comfort-defying leader garners appreciation, trust, and loyalty. How are you doing on this?

Here are a few ideas to help you jump-start your battle against the comfort zone.

Show Up. Life is full of milestones, many of them seemingly insignificant. However, we don't want to miss the opportunities life presents regularly to show up for people. This sounds easy, yet for some, it will be hard. Showing up could take you out of your comfort zone, and that's okay. There's a lot of good outside your normal behaviors.

As we thought about when we've shown up for those we were in community with, Mark recalled the story of showing up at a friend's son's junior varsity football debut. One of Mark's team members had been talking for a long time about his son playing JV football. So, when the day finally came, Mark was preparing to leave the office early when someone asked him where he was going. He told them he was headed to a JV football game.

"Is your son playing?"

"No, I'm going to support a friend."

He wasn't even sure if the kid would play, but Mark wanted to show up to show his support. This was a big deal to his friend, and therefore, it was a big deal for Mark. What would his role be? All he wanted to do was give the gift of presence—and hugs at the end of the game.

Where can you show up for members of your team? Where can they show up for each other?

Celebrate Often. Does your team celebrate enough? Most don't. You need to celebrate more. As we mentioned in the chapter on Team Basics, if you have performance goals and a scorecard, you're more likely to identify legitimate opportunities to say "Well done" to the entire team. If you want to Do Life Together, one path is celebration. Have you ever considered all the things you could celebrate? Here are a few ideas:

- Completing an advanced degree
- Promotion to a new role
- Completion of a significant project
- Child getting their driver's license
- Buying a first home
- Birthdays
- Engagements
- Receiving a new certification
- Employment milestone
- Completing a marathon
- Invitation to speak at an industry event
- Finishing a remodeling project
- Child's acceptance to college
- Completing a passion project
- Publishing a book
- Selling a first painting

How can you celebrate your individual team members?

Mourn with Them. After the horrific attacks on 9/11, former New York City Mayor Rudy Giuliani attended a lot of funerals. He had an intuitive sense that informed his actions in the aftermath of the tragedy. Years later, when he reflected on his experience, he said, "Weddings are optional, funerals are mandatory."[6]

If you really want to Do Life Together, it's great to celebrate, but you have to do the hard stuff too. Everyone you know and every one of your team members will encounter times of pain and hardship. Count on it. Don't miss these opportunities. What do you do? Show up, step out of your comfort zone, and be there. What will you say? Maybe nothing. Your presence speaks volumes.

Mark and some of his friends were in community with a guy whose father had died. Many complicating factors were going to prevent them from being able to attend the funeral. They were heartbroken. So, they did the next best thing they could. They chartered a plane and flew in the night before. They went to the funeral home and hugged their friend. They went back to the airport and flew home. When questioned on the necessity of the trip, their response was, "This is what you do in community. You show up. We had been to the weddings of his daughters—it only felt right to help him bury his dad." When you're in community, you Do Life Together—the weddings *and* the funerals.

PRACTICE!

We know this **Practice!** activity can be a little scary. However, we have 100% confidence in two things. One, you can do this! Two, you'll thank us later. Do something to escape your comfort zone this week and every week.

IS IT LOVE?

We've worked diligently to minimize our sports examples throughout this book. We understand that, in many cases, they can come off sounding like platitudes. We also know many of you didn't grow up participating in team sports. However, we decided to make an exception to our self-imposed limits as we end this chapter.

In January 1986, the Chicago Bears, under the leadership of Mike Ditka, won Super Bowl XX. According to many who follow the sport, this team was the greatest the game of football has ever produced. Here are a few of their key stats:[7, 8]

- Regular Season Record: 15–1
- Playoff Record: 2–0 (before Super Bowl)
- Super Bowl Result: Defeated the New England Patriots 46–10
- Points Scored: 456 (1st in NFL)

- Points Allowed: 198 (1st in NFL)
- Total Yards Offense: 5,837 (2nd in NFL)
- Total Yards Defense: 4,135 (1st in NFL)
- Takeaways: 54 (1st in NFL)
- Sacks: 64 (1st in NFL)
- Pro Bowl Players: 9

Years later, while doing a television interview, Ditka was asked why he thought the '85 Bears were so great. We remember hearing his response and marveling at his clarity and simplicity. He said, "Those guys learned to work together, and they learned how to love each other." Several things stand out to us today as we replay his comment decades later.

"Work together" sounds a lot like the Team Basics we described in our previous chapter. And could "love each other" be describing community? Is love the real output of a place where people know each other deeply, serve each other willingly, and Do Life Together? Perhaps.

Whether you want to call this love or not is irrelevant. What matters is that you work to create an incredibly special place for your team—we call it *community*. The other notable facet of Ditka's response is that he said the team *learned* to do these things. Your team can learn them too. All they need is a leader to show them the way.

Lead Every Day Operating System

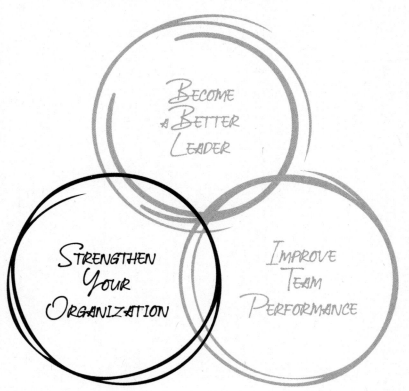

Become a Better Leader

Strengthen Your Organization

Improve Team Performance

STRENGTHEN YOUR ORGANIZATION

The purpose of an organization is to enable common men to do uncommon things.
—Peter Drucker

Why does your organization exist? Our assumption is you want to produce something and sell it for a profit. If you are leading in a nonprofit organization, we would assume you are trying to produce something that enriches the lives of others. We also assume you have rallied others to help you do your thing—for profit, for humanity, or both. The principles and practices we're about to reveal will work equally as well whether you are selling widgets or preventing diseases. Your product may be a service, a cure, or even eyeglasses for a developing country.

This third discipline in our Operating System is the final one you'll need to master if you want to maximize your contribution to the world, regardless of how you measure success. In the first two disciplines, we explored specific strategies and tactics to Become a Better Leader and Improve Team Performance. Now we turn our attention to how you can Strengthen Your Organization.

When you see the title of this section, some of you may be asking several thoughtful questions. *But wait, I'm not the CEO or on*

*the senior leadership team. Isn't this section for them? Why do I need this
content? Why isn't it enough for me to just Become a Better Leader and
Improve Team Performance?*

Great questions! We believe every leader at every level should
be actively contributing to the overall success of the organization
at large. Only through the collective efforts of all leaders, and ultimately every employee, can your organization become a High
Performance Organization. Yes, you must execute on your daily
responsibilities to lead whatever has been entrusted to you—the
first two disciplines addressed those directly. But you also have
the opportunity every day to help your organization do something great. In this section, we'll outline the key strategies you'll
need to Strengthen Your Organization. To set the stage, let's turn
the clock back a few years and share a story.

Mark and his team had been working for years to help their
organization learn and apply the content in the previous section.
They had been focused on helping leaders significantly improve
the performance of their teams. In a long-range planning meeting,
the senior team was wrestling with a familiar question: "What do
we want to be true in a decade that's not true today?"

Mark drew the following diagram on a flip chart.

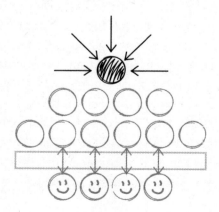

Here's the narrative that accompanied the artwork. "This image represents the simplified structure of a typical CFA restaurant. The smiling faces are the customers on the other side of the front counter.

"For many years, our strategy was to provide growth opportunities for the point leader [he or she is the one at the top of the pyramid represented by the shaded circle]. This worked fine for several decades. However, as the business grew in volume and complexity, we began to see the real leadership capacity constraints of a single leader.

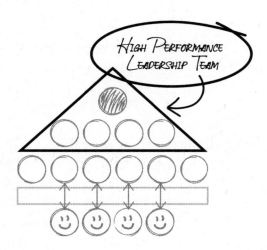

"To combat this, we began to encourage the Operators to consider building a leadership team [the leadership team is represented by the triangle at the top of the pyramid].

"As you know, this has worked spectacularly well. When the Operator builds a team [using the content from the previous section], sales, profits, customer satisfaction, and other key health indicators skyrocket.

"However, here's the dark side of a High Performance

Leadership Team: Fundamentally, all you've done is harness the talent, passion, energy, and creativity of four or five people. Don't get me wrong—this is amazing for the business!

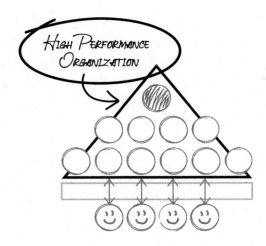

"As we look to the next decade, I think the real opportunity is to encourage Operators to build their own High Performance Organization (HPO)." [represented by the larger triangle encompassing the *entire* team].

"Just imagine the untapped potential in the hundreds of thousands of hourly employees who don't sit around a leadership table. How do we harness the talent, passion, energy, and creativity of all those people? That's what I'd like to see be true in a decade that's not true today."

As Mark finished, he admits, he felt good about this vision. When he turned to take his seat, his boss, who was the team leader and the soon-to-be president of the company, said, "I've got just one question . . . Do you know how to build a High Performance Organization?"

Mark confessed, "I have no idea."

The boss said, "You better figure it out because that's what we're going to do."

As had been Mark's pattern throughout his career, he assembled a talented team of individuals to help answer the question, "How do you build a High Performance Organization?"

After several years of research, benchmarking, and a pilot with their own restaurants, they cracked the code. Here's a summary of what all great organizations do: They Bet on Leadership, Act as One, Win the Heart, and Excel at Execution.

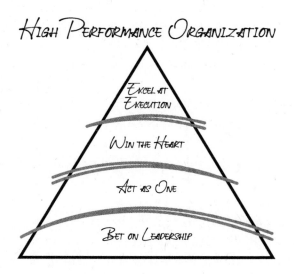

The balance of this section will allow us to give you a deep dive into the four moves all High Performance Organizations make. (The reference to "moves" is a nod to the book *Chess Not Checkers* where we first published these ideas.)

A word about words. In the chapters that follow, we've modified the language above. Yes, the picture we've created does accurately depict the four ever-present strategies you'll find in all

High Performance Organizations. However, we knew we needed to personalize these descriptors and translate them so that every leader, regardless of level, title, or seniority, understood their individual opportunity and responsibility to contribute to the overall health, vitality, and strength of their organization. As mentioned a few pages back, we believe every leader has an essential role to play in your organization's quest for high performance. Therefore, we've translated these four moves into actions every leader can take every day. You must Develop More Leaders, Build the Culture, Increase Engagement, and Focus on Execution. Through your individual actions in these crucial areas, you will enable your organization to join the ranks of the elite. Your business or non-profit can become a High Performance Organization.

Develop More Leaders. Everything rises and falls on leadership. After our extensive efforts to discern what all great organizations have in common, this was our first conclusion: We can't find a High Performance Organization (HPO) on the planet that is not well-led.

Build the Culture. The second move of HPOs is their relentless focus on alignment. Although there are many levers a leader can pull to enhance alignment, the most far-reaching tool at a leader's disposal is the culture. Every organization has a culture, either by design or default, and leaders decide which path they will take.

Increase Engagement. Next, all HPOs know the importance of engagement. According to ADP, based on their global survey of employees in 19 countries, only 15% are fully engaged at work.[1] How does this translate practically to the day-to-day operations of an enterprise? The painful truth is these disengaged people just don't care—they don't care about their work, their coworkers, their customers, or the company. In the best organizations, swimming against the current of this global malady and creating a highly engaged workforce is a priority.

Focus on Execution. Finally, as important as the first three moves are, in HPOs leaders understand that those moves are enablers. The ultimate goal is sustained levels of elite performance. This is only possible when the organization is always in pursuit of a single standard: Do the right thing, the right way, every time. This is the essence of elite execution.

In this final section, we'll help you chart the course to build your own High Performance Organization. Get ready for the ride of your life!

DEVELOP MORE LEADERS

Come work with us, and you'll get a PhD in football.
—Bill Walsh

What is the number one factor holding organizations back? What's undermining all the hopes, dreams, and aspirations of shareholders, board members, senior leaders, and employees? We're not talking about your organization—think globally. Is there a root cause for the malaise so many organizations are experiencing? From our perspective, the answer is a resounding *yes*!

As we mentioned in the introduction, we've conducted a lot of research over the years. One of our more insight-rich surveys was focused on the topic of leadership. Our work with over 4,000 participants from five countries revealed a shocking reality: 30% of organizations don't have enough leaders, and 50% don't believe they will ever solve this problem. This is unacceptable! You cannot, you will not, build a High Performance Organization without a ready supply of qualified leaders. Leaders are the foundation of all great organizations.[1]

Now, at the risk of creating what appears to be a contradiction, there is something every organization needs more than leadership—they need a *leadership culture*. A leadership culture is a place where leaders are routinely and systematically developed and you have a surplus.

Before we get emails and text messages challenging the part about having a surplus of leaders, we'll deal with that question now. The reason you need a surplus is because that is the only indication your process is working. And, you don't know when your next problem to solve or opportunity to seize is coming. You don't want to be caught short. As a wise man once said, "Dig your well before you're thirsty." This is exactly what you want to do. Your future is literally riding on this one simple question: *Can you develop enough leaders to make your aspirations a reality?* This was the question one of our clients asked a few years ago.

Snellings Walters Insurance Agency (SWIA), founded in 1952, sells business insurance and simplifies employee benefits. Their leadership made a decision a few years ago to double the size of their agency in five years. Their goal: move from $15 million a year to $30 million in annual revenue.

The leadership team acknowledged the number one problem would be developing enough leaders to accommodate the growth while ensuring a values-based culture. Over the last four years, SWIA has embraced the Lead Every Day Operating System. The principles, practices, and disciplined approach to training brought structure and purpose to the organization's leadership development efforts.

As of this writing, the company is within striking distance of hitting their revenue targets early and have doubled the number of employees. In addition to the sales increases, SWIA has been recognized by their industry and their employees as a great place to work. Most recently, SWIA was named the best mid-sized business in Atlanta.

THE GENIUS

Who's the smartest person in the room? It's probably not who you think. The answer is often not related to their IQ or educational pedigree. It's the person who can Develop More Leaders. If you want to know the future of your team, division, or entire organization, just look at your leadership bench. How many ready-now leaders do you have? Regardless of your answer today, with focused effort, you can literally change your destiny and impact future generations of your organization and perhaps your industry—maybe even the world. One of the most public illustrations of this is former San Francisco 49ers head football coach Bill Walsh.

After more than 20 years of coaching in high school and college and serving as an assistant in the professional ranks, Walsh became the head coach and general manager of the San Francisco 49ers in 1979. His on-the-field accomplishments were spectacular. During his nine years with the team, they won three Super Bowls (XVI, XIX, and XXIII) and six NFC West Division Titles. He built one of the sport's great dynasties. This part of Walsh's résumé is well known. What is less discussed is the legacy he left behind in the sport he loved.[2]

In his relatively short NFL coaching career, Walsh was doing much more than winning championships. He was also quietly conducting a master class on how to Develop More Leaders—not just any leaders, but men who would reach the pinnacle of their sport.

At last count, more than twenty NFL head coaches, nine assistant coaches, five general managers, and one team president are the direct descendants of Walsh's tree. His "descendants" have won fourteen Super Bowls. If you look at Coach Walsh's track record of success as a coach and his legacy, as demonstrated by those he developed performing at the highest levels of their sport, you can probably understand why many who knew Bill called him "the Genius."

BUILD YOUR OWN LEADERSHIP CULTURE

Okay, you may be thinking, *Developing More Leaders sounds great, and I'd love to be the genius in the room, but you guys don't understand my organization or my industry.* You are correct—we don't—but principles are transferable. There are seven principle-based and time-tested steps you can take to Develop More Leaders. Let's jump in!

#1 Define Leadership

What's your organization's definition of leadership? The biggest mistake we have seen leaders make in organizations around the world who say they want to develop leaders is their failure to define leadership. If you don't have an agreed-upon definition of leadership, is it any wonder you can't Develop More Leaders? In our survey, about 60% of global leaders said they have a common, working definition of leadership. If you are among this group, congratulations . . . maybe.

In the same survey, when we asked frontline leaders if their organization had a common definition of leadership, 72% said they did not know if they did or not.[3] The lesson here: If you do have a shared definition, that's a great start. However, your work is just beginning. You need to work through the following steps to ensure you have successfully cascaded your definition and the requisite skills to every leader at every level. Remember, those leaders closest to the front line have a disproportionate influence on the performance of your organization. Senior leaders don't make the products or serve your customers; the frontline people do. If they are not well-led, you can forget sustained levels of elite performance. Any vision of high performance is nothing more than the delusions of out-of-touch leadership.

So, you may be wondering, *How do we define leadership?* Great question! You only have a couple of options.

You can create your own definition of leadership. This is the path Chick-fil-A took more than 25 years ago. We'll share their point of view momentarily. For those of you considering this path, we have a few tips.

- **Think behaviorally.** Many definitions of leadership are conceptual, theoretical, or abstract. There is probably truth in all of them. However, you are trying to inform and instruct your leaders on how to behave. When someone sees your definition, it should help them know what to do.
- **Keep it simple.** The more elaborate your definition, the less effective it will be. You need your leadership point of view to be an ever-present companion for your leaders, simple enough to be applied in the rigor of day-to-day life.
- **Avoid multiple definitions.** Many organizations have different definitions of leadership for various levels of leadership. This is a level of complexity you don't need. If you are thoughtful, you can create a single definition that works across levels. The difference will be in time horizon and application.

You can use someone else's definition. There are thousands of existing definitions to choose from. Here's the one we developed at Chick-fil-A 25 years ago. We have identified five fundamentals of Uncommon Leaders:

See the Future
Engage and Develop Others
Reinvent Continuously
Value Results and Relationships
Embody a Leader's Heart

Note: We covered Chick-fil-A's definition of leadership in greater detail in the earlier chapter entitled "Learn the Fundamentals" and we go even deeper in the book Uncommon Greatness.

Regardless of whether you create your own definition or use someone else's, choose wisely. This is a decision that has the potential to mark your organization for decades. You really do need to get this right.

We're from Atlanta. The Braves are our baseball team. They have certainly had their ups and downs over the years, including winning the World Series in 1995 and 2021. However, they also have a rather dubious record that comes to mind when thinking about this first step in the process of making more leaders.

If you're a baseball fan, you may have heard the saying "You can't win the game in the first inning, but you can certainly lose it there." Well, the Atlanta Braves tried to test this axiom in the 2019 playoffs—Randy was in the ballpark that day for a deciding game against the St. Louis Cardinals. Unfortunately, it wasn't much of a game. The Braves gave up 10 runs in the first inning. The final score was 13–1, but the game was lost in the first inning.[4]

Not to be outdone, in the 2021 playoffs, the Braves were scheduled to play the LA Dodgers. Mark was present for this postseason showdown between two of the best teams in the league. Tragically, if you were a Braves fan, the team gave up 11 runs in the first inning. You guessed it—they lost the game. The Braves are now known as the only team in baseball history to give up 10+ runs in the first inning of two playoff games. Maybe we shouldn't go to any more playoff games!

What does this have to do with making more leaders? Everything! You can't win the game by creating your definition of leadership, but you'll lose the game if you don't. This is the first step for a reason. If you don't want to do Step One, save your energy and effort; don't waste your time on the steps that follow.

PRACTICE!

If your team or organization doesn't already have a working definition of leadership, start the process within the next 30 days. Schedule the time and begin the work. Don't be surprised if this is a very time-consuming project. Think months, not weeks. You really do want to get this right for your organization. Your definition should have an enduring quality.

#2 Name Your Leadership Champion

Who is going to think about developing leaders more than the point leader does? As the world and our organizations grow in complexity, specialization has become the norm. Just look at the way organizations have evolved over the years. Many of the roles in the modern organization didn't exist just a few years ago.

Imagine the leadership team at a typical fast-food restaurant. At Chick-fil-A, just a few years ago, leadership teams didn't even exist in these restaurants. Back then, a single highly capable individual—known as the Operator—ran the entire operation.

These Operators were the driving force behind every decision, managing every detail themselves.

But as business grew and the complexity of operations increased, so did the need for specialization. The responsibilities became too much for one person to handle alone. The Operator, still the independent businessperson at the helm, began bringing in others to help. While the roles vary from location to location, it's now common to see someone focused on marketing, another on quality, another on training. Others take charge of food safety, drive-throughs, catering, and talent management.

In fact, many locations have gone a step further, adding a Leadership Champion to oversee the development of current and future leaders. It's a big shift from just a few years ago, and a sign of how much these restaurants have grown and adapted to meet new demands.

How do you know if you need a Leadership Champion? Three questions will probably provide enough information for you to decide. "How competent are your existing leaders? How deep is your leadership bench?" The answers will help you quantify the magnitude of the challenge you face.

If your leaders need more development than they are receiving today and/or you don't have leaders in waiting, you probably need a champion to give this critical gap more attention. This may or may not be a full-time position based on your current circumstances. However, if a gap exists, it will not rectify itself. When your current structure is not allowing you to do what needs to be done, change it.

The final question is, "Are you willing and able to add the following responsibilities to *your* job description?" If not, name a Leadership Champion—someone has to own this critical role in a growing organization with their sights set on greatness.

What does a Leadership Champion do? Here are some ideas:

- Keep the topic of leadership development on the leadership team's agenda at all times.
- Facilitate the process of creating your definition of leadership (if you don't already have one).
- Create or select the training materials and resources you'll use with your leaders.
- Ensure ongoing leadership training is delivered with excellence.
- Help leaders create Individual Development Plans.
- Meet with leaders periodically to check on their progress.
- Work with the leadership team to evaluate the efficacy of your training and development efforts.
- Assist the leadership team as they match mentors with mentees.
- Maintain your leadership scorecard.
- Facilitate formal leadership review sessions with the leadership team.

As you can see from the simple abbreviated job description, the role of the champion is multifaceted.

In summary:

The Leadership Champion is the person who will build, operate, and maintain your leadership engine.

We want to challenge you to think carefully about this step in the process. This may be the most strategic decision you'll ever make as a leader. Your ability to accomplish your hopes and dreams for your organization rests on your ability to Develop More Leaders. We believe the champion's role is indispensable.

┌─ **PRACTICE!** ─────────────────────┐

Modify the job description above as needed, seek wise
counsel from members of your team, assign this role to
someone already on your payroll, or begin recruiting
today. If you don't have the resources, you'll need to step
in and fill this role. It is far too important to leave the position vacant.

└──────────────────────────────┘

#3 Set Your Leadership Goals

Specifically, what are you trying to accomplish in the area of leadership? Of course, you'll continue to have goals in other areas of
your business. Goals drive performance. This is not a new idea for
leaders. Ironically, many organizations have no goals pertaining
to leadership. If you want to Develop More Leaders, you probably
need a few goals in this arena. Here are a few examples to stimulate your thinking:

- If you don't have a common definition of leadership,
  establish one by a certain date.
- Designate your Leadership Champion.
- How many open leadership positions do you have today?
  Set a goal to begin closing the gap.
- How many ready-now leaders do you have (a metric of
  bench strength)? How many do you want and by when?

┌─ **PRACTICE!** ─────────────────────┐

Set three to five near-term goals in the leadership arena.
Be prepared to set new ones after you accomplish the initial set.

└──────────────────────────────┘

#4 Build Your Leadership Scorecard

What metrics will you use to monitor your progress? We've been asked why this step is different from the previous one regarding leadership goals. Admittedly, there can be overlap. However, some of your goals will look more like Action Items (e.g., name a Leadership Champion by year-end). A scorecard is comprised of metrics deserving ongoing monitoring and attention. Don't be surprised if you ultimately decide to include some of your goals on your scorecard in order to drive improvement.

Here are a few examples of items you may decide to include on your scorecard depending on the needs of your team/organization:

- Percentage of our leaders who have been trained on our leadership definition.
- Number of open leadership positions.
- Number, or percentage, of leaders who have an Individual Development Plan.
- A metric associated with leadership effectiveness. Here's one approach: If you do an annual engagement survey or organizational health assessment, you can create an index from key attributes to represent the collective performance of your leaders (e.g., if frontline associates say they don't know the vision of the organization, that's a reflection on leadership). You can choose several of these line items and aggregate them to measure leadership efficacy.

How many metrics do you need? Hard to say. You should think about this question the same way you decided on the primary metrics for your team scorecard. However, we are confident the right number of metrics will be focused on a critical few leadership health indicators.

Your leadership scorecard will help you maintain focus, foster accountability, highlight wins and opportunities to celebrate, and identify gaps/problems.

> ## ⌐ PRACTICE! ———
>
> Begin building your scorecard as soon as you have identified your initial goals and named your champion. The champion should lead this effort to create your leadership scorecard.

#5 Train Your Leaders

How will you train your leaders? This is the fun part. It's also where most organizations start the process. Unfortunately, if you began your journey here, chances are high you are dissatisfied with your efforts to date. Without first defining leadership, your efforts cannot be strategic—you are probably guilty of random acts of training. Assuming you now have a definition of leadership, you're ready to begin exploring options for how you'll train your leaders. The following are several ideas for you to consider.

Create Individual Development Plans

We've addressed this idea in several previous chapters, but we want to add a little more color commentary. A key word that is often overlooked here is the word *individual*. The more targeted and personalized a plan can be to maximize impact and accelerate learning, the better. As an example, if someone prefers audiobooks to traditional books, their plan should reflect this. If the person's predominant learning style is kinesthetic—they learn best by doing—their plan should be laden with experiences and project-based learning.

Every plan will have some commonality. If there is a one-day introduction to your leadership point of view, it should be included in every leader's plan. However, once you move past the core curriculum and prescribed content, the plans should truly become individualized. One person will need to improve their listening skills while another will need to work on public speaking. This is the ultimate power behind this tool. Every plan is bespoke. You may be thinking, *That sounds like a heavy lift.* It is. Just one more reason you may want to refer to Step Two. Your champion can not only help build these plans; he or she can have regular check-ins to monitor progress and offer assistance.

Use Projects and Problems

When working to Develop More Leaders, you don't want to miss the fact that as much as 70% of what leaders know about leading, they learned by leading. If you want to accelerate development and tackle some outstanding issues, consider assigning a challenging project or an emerging problem to an existing leader. You can even use this approach with men and women who are not in official positions of leadership.

Johnson & Johnson uses high-stakes, cross-functional projects to develop leadership skills. Leaders and aspiring leaders are placed in charge of "stretch assignments," projects that push them beyond their usual responsibilities and skill sets. This has included leading teams across global markets, innovating product lines, or addressing pressing health challenges.[5]

Make a wish list of projects and problems you'd like to address if you had the necessary leadership capacity. Maybe you want to overhaul your recruiting process or discover why employee turnover is at an all-time high. Perhaps sales are declining on your primary product or service and you really don't know why. Maybe you need a new product offering and no one has time to work on developing one.

If you assign any of these to someone as a developmental opportunity, don't abandon them. If you want to take full advantage of this scenario, you'll want to coach them, check on them, provide appropriate boundaries, and so on. If this sounds like a lot of work, it can be. Your Leadership Champion can help shoulder the load.

Train Job Skills and Leadership Skills

We have encountered our fair share of leaders who think they have a development plan, but they really don't—what they do have is a plan to develop their technical expertise or job skills. This facet of a leader's development is important but totally insufficient for the task ahead.

Every leader, every human for that matter, needs job skills. If you are a plumber, lawyer, doctor, or salesperson, a certain subject matter expertise is required for you to be successful. From time to time, we see leaders who have mistaken their job skills training plan for a leadership development plan. The sales manager probably needs to continue to develop her sales skills, but these skills alone do not make her a leader. The technical aspects of your profession matter—they are one side of the coin. The other side is your leadership competency. Be sure you don't confuse the two.

Leverage Digital Learning

There are dozens of ways to facilitate learning. One approach growing in popularity is digital learning. There are many types/formats/platforms and methodologies. The advantages include personalization, accessibility, interactivity, increased engagement, improved retention of content, cost-effectiveness, gamification, flexibility, and data tracking.

We are huge fans of this strategy! We've created the Lead Every Day Academy, an online and app-based resource with scores of videos, notes, and quizzes to help you learn and apply the Lead Every Day Operating System.

To learn more, go to ***https://www.leadeverydayacademy.com***, *or scan this QR code:*

The items in this section are only intended to stimulate your creativity. You have so many other options! Other methodologies include book studies, classes, outside coaches, peer learning groups, formal education, workshops, conferences, and more.

Here's one additional idea. As part of its efforts to scale leadership development, Google launched a volunteer program called Guru, enabling employees to receive personalized coaching. In this program, employees volunteer as "gurus" and undergo preparatory training to effectively support others. The program uses the GROW coaching model (Goal, Reality, Opportunity, What will you do?), guiding participants toward clear, actionable development opportunities. The result? A network of volunteers providing customized, goal-focused coaching across the organization![6]

By whatever means you can muster, be sure your leaders are trained to execute against *your* definition of leadership as outlined in the first step above.

PRACTICE!

Ask your Leadership Champion to create a first draft of a training plan for some subset of your leaders (e.g., frontline, mid-level, or senior leaders). This assignment assumes you have done the first step and defined leadership. If you haven't already begun training leaders, we would suggest you not conduct any sessions until after you've completed Step One. Then, train your first cohort and see what you learn.

#6 Evaluate Your Leaders

How well are your current leaders performing? Organizations that Develop More Leaders are intentional regarding the evaluation of their existing leaders. There are many ways to do this, but we're fans of keeping things simple. To that end, we recommend a four-box with the *y*-axis representing the performance of the leader and the *x*-axis representing their leadership competency (as evaluated against your definition of leadership).

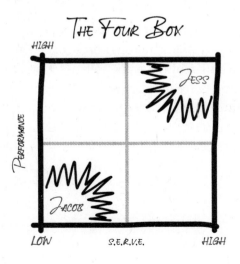

The process is straightforward. You assemble the right group of people. In most cases, this will be the leadership team. You discuss each leader, asking and answering two questions: How is their performance? How is their leadership? You work to reach a consensus by asking for examples and illustrations to accurately position someone on the four-box. High performance and high leadership competency lands someone in the upper right-hand quadrant. Poor performance and poor leadership would position someone in the lower left quadrant.

You will accomplish a couple of things when you go through this exercise. First, you will calibrate on what superior performance and good leadership looks like. This is extremely valuable. Before you had a common definition of leadership, an exercise like this would be a work of pure fiction. Without an agreed-upon standard, qualities such as personality, politics, or position would prevail over the actual competency of the leader being assessed. What happens next is transformational.

After you plot all the leaders on your four-box, you begin round two. Look at the upper right and lower left quadrants. In both cases, you are working to determine what's next for these individuals. The lower left employees are in jeopardy. You cannot allow them to remain in leadership if they stay in the lower left corner. So, the conversation should revolve around what can be done to help this person move up and to the right. Once you agree on next steps, their IDP is adjusted accordingly.

For the people in the top right box, you are considering what's next for them. Do they need a promotion? More responsibility? Perhaps a new role? How do we best steward this star performer? Is there a project or problem we want to assign to them? Whatever is decided, their IDP should be updated accordingly.

The final step is to look at leaders in the other two quadrants—what can you do to help them continue to improve?

The four-box is just one approach to evaluate your leaders. Any method you choose should help you answer the question, "What can you do to help your leaders grow?"

> ## ⎡ PRACTICE! ⎤
>
> Schedule time with your leadership team to begin the review process. You can ask your Leadership Champion to facilitate the meeting.

#7 Improve and Repeat the Process

How will you improve the process (Steps One through Six)? Our seventh step is the key to sustainability. The seventh step transforms a short-term project into a perpetual motion machine. As you review your implementation of the previous steps, you'll note some of them may need a bit of reinvention while others are perfectly suitable for the next cycle. Here are six questions to help you jump-start Step Seven:

1. **Define Leadership**
    What refinements, if any, does your definition of leadership need?
2. **Name Your Leadership Champion**
    What adjustments do you need to make to your champion's job description?
3. **Set Your Leadership Goals**
    If you've accomplished your initial leadership goals, what goals should you set next?
4. **Build Your Leadership Scorecard**
    What adjustments, if any, do you need to make to your leadership scorecard?

5. **Train Your Leaders**

   What have you learned thus far that will enable you to improve the effectiveness of future training?

6. **Evaluate Your Leaders**

   Based on your most recent assessment of your leaders, what can you do to make your next round of reviews more effective?

PRACTICE!

Periodically, you and your leadership team need to ask and answer this question: What will we do to improve our process for Developing More Leaders? Our suggestion is that you do this at least once a year. As you build your planning calendar for next year, why not make this part of your process?

JUST IMAGINE

Just imagine what you and your organization could do with more leaders. Think of the projects you could tackle and the problems you could address. What about growth? You'll never outgrow your leadership.

We are thankful for the opportunity we've had over the years to teach leaders from scores of countries around the world the ideas in this book. We've seen firsthand the universal power released when organizations are well-led.

On his first trip to Indonesia, Mark met a former engineer who in his midlife career change decided to become a pastor. When Niko Njotorahardjo started the church in the early '90s, the congregation quickly grew to become a thriving church with 500 people in their weekly services. The day Mark sat down with the pastor more than 20 years into his tenure, they were averaging *500,000* in attendance.

"How is this possible?" Mark asked.

"Which part?" Niko responded.

"How did you go from 500 to 500,000?"

"I learned to lead. When I learned to lead, we began to grow. Then, I taught others to lead. Today, we have 1,000 congregations, each averaging 500 in attendance per week." Mark's visit was just their most recent effort to invest in their leaders. Quarterly leadership training was part of their normal routine.

What would happen if you could Become a Better Leader, Improve Team Performance, and Strengthen Your Organization? What would happen if you taught every leader in your organization to do the same?

Pastor Niko is not an isolated case. Yes, his success has been breathtaking; however, we are thankful to report hundreds of thousands—honestly, millions—of people who have already been impacted by the content you are exploring in this book. Our heartfelt desire is for you to join the ranks of leaders who have experienced firsthand the power unleashed when you Develop More Leaders.

BUILD THE CULTURE

When you align the entire organization around a clear and
inspiring vision, incredible things can happen.
—Jack Welch

How important is culture, really? We asked leaders around the world about the drivers of performance and 67% said culture was the most powerful tool at their disposal to drive performance. Nothing ranked higher (71% of US leaders rated culture as the number one driver of performance).[1] Unfortunately, the follow-up question revealed why so many organizations struggle with culture and why it has become a liability of untold proportions.

We asked the same leaders to rank their priorities. In the United States, building and maintaining culture came in at number *12*. Ouch! Globally, the ranking was not much better; these leaders ranked this critical task as number *11* on their to-do list. We don't know about you, but we rarely work on our 11th or 12th priority.[2]

THE CHALLENGE OF CULTURE

What's going on here? Leaders, perhaps more than anyone else, care about performance. Leaders told us culture was their number one tool to drive performance, yet they aren't working on it. Why not? Our team explored this question in depth. There are a few plausible reasons this massive misalignment exists.

One, leaders are too consumed by the quicksand of busyness, distraction, complexity, interruptions, fear, fatigue, and, in some cases, success. When leaders are in quicksand, they are not working on culture; they are in survival mode. We discussed the way out of the quagmire in the chapter "Improve Your Effectiveness." If resurfacing the topic of quicksand hits a nerve, please go back and review that chapter.

For those still struggling with the ravages of quicksand, we'll offer one more word of encouragement to get out. If you are in quicksand, you cannot help those around you escape the same fate. Therefore, there is a really good chance the leaders around you are stuck in the same toxic mess you are. Only when you escape can you assist them. Get back to the high ground as quickly as you possibly can.

The second reason this knowing/doing gap persists is that culture can feel really soft. Keep in mind, it is invisible, yet still impacts every decision and action an organization takes. And, to make matters worse, there isn't really a common and pragmatic definition. So, to make culture more tangible and manageable, we wrote one.

Culture is the cumulative effect of what people see, hear, experience, and believe.

We like this definition because leaders are perfectly and uniquely positioned to influence what people see, hear, experience, and believe.

Finally, and probably the greatest impediment to leaders engaging in culture craft: They don't know what to do to build and sustain culture. This issue ultimately became the focus of our multi-year, multimillion-dollar study of organizational culture.

THE CULTURE RULES

Once we exited the research phase, our team's challenge was clear. How do we translate all we have learned from listening to thousands of leaders and individual contributors from around the world and the scores of interviews we did with experts, thought leaders, and practitioners into something useful? More specifically, how do we determine the irreducible minimum contribution a leader must make to create the culture their organization needs? What are the rules of the game? We knew we had to strive for simplicity without becoming simplistic. We found our inspiration for our next steps in an unlikely place: the Navy SEALs.

In 2005, the SEALs were updating their ethos. Former SEAL Brent Gleeson described the situation his leadership team faced: "We had been moving at the speed of war for four years and eventually realized that we had never really defined (on paper) who we are, what we stand for and why we exist."[3]

We think this was clearly a leadership moment for the SEALs. These guys realized they needed to capture what was important for the next generation of warriors. Their final product was a document with many tenets. The first on their list: "Shoot, Move, Communicate."[4]

Why do these three simple words add value? Certainly, they do not encompass all the SEALs need to know or do to be successful, but from this starting point they can engage and prevail in battle. Shoot, Move, Communicate is a powerful mantra because it's clear, succinct, directive, actionable, and it works!

Our team went to work to create similar guidance for leaders when faced with the challenge of creating and sustaining a High Performance Culture. We were searching for something with the same level of clarity, direction, and efficacy. The result—three culture rules:

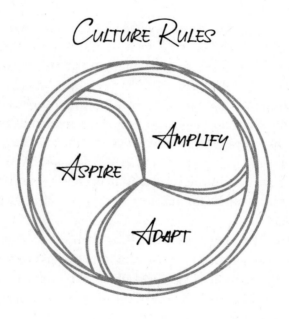

Rule #1

ASPIRE

Share your hopes and dreams for the culture.

To be fully transparent, our team debated whether or not this first rule was too obvious. We weren't sure we needed to tell leaders to start with the end in mind. At some level, we felt this might be insulting. We hope not. We decided we had no choice but to begin here because so many leaders have not told those they serve what they are trying to create. The first rule, Aspire, requires you as the leader to share your hopes and dreams for the culture.

Creating a High Performance Culture is about turning aspiration into reality. Leaders must remember that you are the key drivers and influencers of culture, but you cannot do it alone. Only when you can rally enough people to join you in pursuit of the aspiration does your preferred culture begin to take shape. If you cannot articulate what you are trying to create, the chances of creating it are virtually zero. The exception may be in some extremely small organizations where the leader's proximity to the people is such that individuals can discern their leader's intent. This approach is a high-risk play that requires those around the leader to be mind readers.

The surest path to creating a High Performance Culture begins with sharing your hopes and dreams. However, as we mentioned, many leaders have not done this. Some will insist the picture of the preferred future is clear in their heart or their head—fantastic! That's where aspirations are born. However, the aspiration cannot stay in your head if you want it to grow, mature, and impact the daily behaviors of your organization. You must tell others.

Before we talk about how to craft a compelling aspiration, we want to digress a bit. We've used the term *High Performance Culture* a few times. Let's define that term.

For an organization to have a High Performance Culture, three things must be true:

Alignment: The vast majority of people associated with the organization must voluntarily and wholeheartedly commit to the enterprise's aspirations. The more people who enroll, the stronger the culture will be.

Performance: Every organization has its own metrics of success. Whether leading in a business, the not-for-profit sector, higher education, government, faith-based organizations, or the military, *high performance* will be defined differently in each sphere. Regardless of your definition of success, High Performance Cultures produce superior results over time. Greatness hinges on execution, and culture is the oil for the hinge.

Improvement: There must be an ongoing effort to improve the culture. An organization clinging doggedly to the past may shine brightly for a season, but it will not last. Is your culture getting better? Building a High Performance Culture requires constant vigilance and effort.

Craft the Aspiration

Leadership always begins with a picture of the future, and so does culture. Anytime a leader is creating the future, their talents, gifts, experience, intuition, creativity, imagination, and courage collide. The result: new levels of clarity about your preferred future—your organization's North Star. We addressed crafting your aspiration in the chapter "Learn the Fundamentals" under the banner of "See the Future," but here, we want to take you deeper.

One of the leaders we coach had an all-too-familiar experience with this practice. As described to us by one of his senior leaders, they "fought over the aspiration." The junior leader pinpointed accurately that the lack of buy-in evident in their business stemmed from the lack of clarity regarding the goal—the team did not understand who they were trying to become and what they were trying to create. The senior leader initially believed things were good because sales were still increasing. However, his leaders knew a cultural storm was brewing. The senior leader also thought the aspiration was clear because it was clear to *him*. However, the team was not aligned. We want to give full credit to the senior leader for ultimately listening to the leaders around him.

After a tremendous amount of work, the leadership team relaunched the vision and mission for the business. They described this moment as "catalytic." They are now making many necessary changes so they can achieve their shared vision. The leader who shared this story said, previously, "They were striving; now they are thriving!"

On the following pages, we'll share several tools you can use to create your own guiding light for the people in your organization. We can provide the tools; you must provide the raw materials and the effort.

One more word about the tools. You don't have to use them all. Some will choose to do so, but many will select only one, or a couple, of the following to help them create their own unique picture of a preferred future.

Vision: The Big Picture

Vision is a broad and directional picture of the future. Of all the different mechanisms for articulating the aspiration, vision statements are the most likely to inspire and encourage people. Unfortunately, many vision statements are too technical and precise to inspire. In many cases, they also try to say too much. A great vision statement captures the essence of your aspiration, not the details.

Here are some questions that will help you discover your unique vision for your organization:

- What difference do you want to make in the world?

- What are you convinced your organization should endlessly and tirelessly strive for?
- What is big enough that you could work toward it your entire career and then pass the baton to others to pursue?
- What is so big and so admirable you can think of nothing better to devote your leadership energy toward accomplishing?
- What is something you feel must be passionately pursued?

Mission: The Next Mountain to Climb

Some organizations use a different tool to convey their preferred future—mission. Although there is no consensus surrounding the definitions of any of the aspiration-related tools we're discussing in this section, we've chosen the traditional connotation for mission: a long-term goal, often a goal with significant challenges associated with its achievement.

The quintessential example is President Kennedy's call to put men on the moon and return them safely to Earth before the end of the decade. The year was 1961 and the technology to accomplish the president's mission did not yet exist. However, with the help of over 400,000 dedicated men and women, NASA completed the mission when the astronauts splashed down safely in the Pacific Ocean on July 24, 1969.[5]

Could a mission help you articulate your aspiration? Perhaps. Here are a few questions to help you sort through this:

- What advantages would you anticipate if your entire organization had its version of a "moonshot"?
- What could you strive for in the mid-term future that, if achieved, would have a multiplier effect in your organization?

- What goal could you establish to create a positive ripple effect on your entire organization?
- What goal is so big from today's perspective that you might deem it impossible?
- To what extent would your organization be energized by a bold and challenging long-term goal?

Purpose: Why Your Organization Exists

Many organizations find power and energy in a clearly articulated purpose. Let's get real. There are infinite things leaders cannot know. However, one of the things that is knowable is why your organization exists. A clearly articulated purpose will leave no doubt in the hearts and minds of your employees as to why the work they do matters.

For many people, purpose, a clear statement of why, provides an emotional and intellectual anchor. An organization's purpose can change, but it is typically the most steadfast of all the terms used to articulate the aspiration. This stability is often born of an unshakable resolve in an unchanging motivation. Goals, strategies, and tactics evolve, but purpose is generally held as a constant.

Use these questions to begin mining for your purpose.

- What was your organization born to do?
- What fires you up about the future you are trying to create?
- What do you want the legacy of your organization to be 100 years from now?
- How would you explain why your organization exists (not what you do) to a small child?
- If your organization went away, what would the world lose?

Values: Beliefs That Drive Behavior

The final mechanism we'll explore is values. Simply stated, values represent the way the organization wants people to think and behave.

Prior to 2017, United Airlines operated under the guiding principles of "Fly Right, Fly Friendly, Fly Together, and Fly Above and Beyond." While these values emphasized customer service and operational excellence, they lacked the clarity needed to guide employees' daily actions in critical situations. This ambiguity became evident through several incidents, including the infamous case of a passenger's guitar being broken and the company's insufficient response. Then, in April 2017, when a passenger, Dr. David Dao, was forcibly dragged off a United flight, it caused a major public relations disaster.[6]

The Dr. Dao incident shed light on the airline's internal issues, particularly the disconnect between its stated values and the behaviors exhibited by its employees during high-pressure situations. While United's values aimed to deliver exceptional service, they did not offer employees clear guidance on how to act in difficult or unpredictable scenarios.

In response to the public outcry and internal reflection, United Airlines recognized the need to redefine its values with a focus on clearer behavioral guidelines. By late 2017, the company introduced its Core4 values: Safe, Caring, Dependable, and Efficient.[7]

The results: Honestly, it's probably too soon to call, but many believe United's new value system is helping the organization rebuild its reputation by refocusing their employees on what matters most.

In addition to establishing leadership expectations and cultural norms, values have several other potential applications:

- Help you know who to recruit and select.
- Accelerate the onboarding and training of new employees.
- Serve as the cornerstone for coaching conversations.
- Anchor performance evaluations.
- Provide meaningful points for recognition.
- Help you identify future leaders.

A quick reminder: In many cases, your values will require you to stretch—this is good! All values are aspirational. You should never stop striving to embody the values and become the person your values describe. Here are a few guidelines to help you craft your values.

Use Simple and Clear Language. Clarity is your friend and a gift that you, as the leader, can give to the organization. The values are intended to inform, not impress. You probably want to express your values using language that requires little explanation. As an example, "innovation" as a value is fairly clear. However, "do good" leaves a lot of room for interpretation and questions. We think provocative and descriptive language is also a good thing—it can conjure up vivid images that can help convey the underlying intent of the value (e.g., "customer obsessed" is stronger than "we value customers"; "radical collaboration" is stronger than "collaboration").

Make Your Values Distinctive. Are there unique attributes of your organization you want to leverage or enhance (e.g., scrappy, courageous, audacious)? If so, these could be candidate values. We are not suggesting excellence or innovation be removed from your list of values. Perhaps if you are manufacturing critical medical implants or if you are a design firm, these could make perfect sense. However, virtually every organization in the world could include excellence and innovation on their list of desired values.

Keep the List Short. The more core values you have, the greater the likelihood they won't add value. We don't think there is a perfect number, but from our experience, the "right" answer is as few as possible. Start your quest with a goal of five or less and see what you can accomplish. One of the benefits of having a shorter list is you increase the likelihood of people actually using the values as a point of reference when making day-to-day decisions.

Stay the Course. If you get the values right, they should stand the test of time. We are not suggesting they will never change. Some of the reasons for changing them: new leadership with a new aspiration, new strategy, new behaviors needed to meet the demands of a changing world, and so on. However, if your values change too often, you will confuse your people and slow your progress toward your aspiration. Strategies and tactics change frequently—values should be much more durable. If your values are seen as disposable or just the flavor of the month, you'll hurt your credibility and undermine your leadership.

PRACTICE!

Decide which of the previous mechanisms you'll employ to share your hopes and dreams (e.g., Vision, Purpose, Mission, Values). Many leaders will use more than one of these. With that decision made, begin capturing your thoughts. Once you have clarity about the culture you are trying to create and can describe it to others, you're ready for the second rule.

Rule #2

AMPLIFY

Ensure the cultural aspiration is reinforced continuously.

Armed with your newly minted North Star and a clear and compelling picture of your culture's preferred future, you may think your work is done. Nothing could be further from the truth. We hate to be the ones to break the news, but chances are extremely high many of the people you lead will be underwhelmed by your new insights about the future.

Is this lack of initial buy-in born of cynicism, past experience, or the tsunami of information inundating them on a daily basis? Maybe the reluctance, and often outright resistance, to the latest "vision" is a combination of all these things. There is so much noise in the modern organization that it's increasingly difficult for new messages to break through. That's why the leader must amplify the aspiration. You must rise above the noise and distractions in the world in which you operate. This is the step in the process where people not only begin to hear the message, but if you do this well, they will start to believe you. When they believe you, they will join you.

The second culture rule is to Amplify. Ensure the cultural aspiration is reinforced continuously. This is the ongoing work of leaders in every organization. Before you begin the process of amplifying the aspiration, it is nothing more than an idea, a dream. It has no teeth, no substance, and no evidence it is real.

IDEO is a global design agency known for its continuing ability to help its clients innovate. Mark first became familiar with the firm when he met their chief technologist at a conference. Mark asked his new acquaintance about his history with the company. He said his first project was the mouse for Apple. What a first project!

Since that day, multiple visits to the firm's Palo Alto headquarters have given us a glimpse behind the curtain. As you might expect, their leaders intentionally amplified their aspiration to enhance their ability to be one of the world's most innovative companies. Here are a few of the elements we would suggest are directly linked to their culture of innovation:

- Collaborative workspaces are utilized to facilitate the creative process.
- Design thinking is taught and practiced to facilitate breakthrough ideas.
- Continuous learning is encouraged to provide the seedbed for new ideas.
- A flat hierarchy is employed to increase speed and ownership.
- Diverse teams are created to maximize impact.
- Human-centered design is the standard.
- Experimentation and rapid prototyping are the expectation.

As you can see from IDEO's example, there are many things an organization can do once they are clear on what they are trying to accomplish, and this is only a partial list of what they've done.

What can you do to amplify your aspiration? We want to give you one specific strategy to start implementing today.

Show the Way

People always watch the leader. What are people learning about your commitment to the aspiration by watching you? Can they sense your passion and resolve to make the aspiration a reality? Does your daily routine reflect the type of culture you say you want to create?

Here's a simple exercise to help you better walk the talk and live the aspiration on a daily basis.

Look Back. Review your calendar for the last 90 days. This needs to be an actual day-by-day, hour-by-hour review. What are you looking for? Two things: When did you do something that specifically showed your commitment to the aspiration? As an example, when you spoke to a group of new employees and you shared all or part of the aspiration—maybe you talked about your organization's core values—great! Give yourself a point. The other thing you're looking for is missed opportunities to amplify the aspiration. Let's say when you spoke to the new employee group, you did not talk about the aspiration. *Subtract* two points. Complete this line-item audit for the previous 90-day period. How did you do? What was your score?

Look Forward. Think of this as an opportunity audit, no scoring required. See how many opportunities you can identify in advance to amplify your cultural aspiration. There will be scores of situations in which you can play your role as chief cultural ambassador. Just to jump-start your thinking, here is a partial list:

- Mentoring an employee
- Talking to customers
- Talking to suppliers
- Designing a training experience
- Meeting one-on-one with a team member
- Meeting with a team
- Conducting a performance review
- Speaking for an outside group
- Talking about the future
- Holding recognition events

- Coaching a team member
- Meeting with your board of directors
- Attending meetings
- Crafting and sending emails

While doing an interview with a CEO for our book *Culture Rules*, we were informed he would need to leave our meeting a little early in order to speak to new employees. Fifteen minutes earlier, he had proudly shared with us the organization's refreshed aspiration, including their new and improved core values. When we offered the assumption that he would share their new aspiration with these team members, he said the thought "never crossed his mind."[8]

Our days are full of opportunities to show people what our aspiration looks like in action. What are people learning about your preferred future by watching you work? Remember, people always watch the leader. When they see us honestly and consistently pursuing the aspiration, they are much more likely to join the cause and become true believers.

PRACTICE!

Have a conversation with your leadership team about the importance of leaders showing others the way. Have each individual reflect on situations from their past when they saw a leader living out their aspiration. Ask the members of the group to share the story and what they were thinking when they witnessed this situation. Also, ask them to share how it made them feel.

Embed the Aspiration

When doing our research on organizational culture, we found the methods to amplify the aspiration fit into two categories: proximal and structural. Our first practice activity above, "Show the Way," is the classic proximal example. If you aren't close enough for people to see you, the impact of your behavior is reduced. The idea of embedding the aspiration is when you do things structurally that will amplify the aspiration. These are mechanisms that work without a leader's physical presence. Examples of this type of amplification include compensation, incentives tied to progress toward the aspiration, and policies that elevate the aspiration.

If your organization aspires to have an impact in your local community, giving your employees paid time to volunteer would amplify your aspiration. Structural considerations—the way teams are organized and spaces are designed—could influence levels of innovation and collaboration. Measurement systems can help you embed the aspiration as well. If you say that you want to be known for innovation, you can build metrics to assess the factors that stimulate or impede new ideas. Never underestimate the impact your systems, processes, and structure have on your culture.

PRACTICE!

Make a list of all the places your systems, structure, and practices are misaligned with your aspiration. Rank them in order of impact on the culture you are trying to create. Begin making plans to address these one by one.

Rule #3

ADAPT

Always work to enhance the culture.

At this point, some of you are wondering why there is a third rule. You assume or have experienced success in the past with the diligent application of the first two rules. They work! Why would you not just stop with two rules? This is a fair question, and the opening premise stated above is correct—if you deliberately and diligently apply the first two rules, you will transform your culture. We understand the temptation to stop there—leaders love to get things done. We get a shot of dopamine when we mark something off our to-do list. Why not just put a big check mark by *culture* and move on to other issues? Because you are not done. If you think you are done, you are really done. If you attempt to simply shrink-wrap your culture to protect and preserve it, you will suffocate it. Culture is comprised of living, breathing human beings. You cannot merely preserve your culture. You must work to make it better. The third culture rule is: Adapt. Always work to enhance the culture.

Yes, working to enhance the culture is a never-ending job, but that's okay. Your desire for results doesn't end either, and we know culture is the number one driver of performance. So, by working on culture, you'll be investing the balance of your career working on the right thing—again, assuming you still care about results.

When you think about enhancing your culture, we want to give you four domains to explore: close critical gaps, eliminate toxins, leverage your strengths, and add new capabilities. If you read *Culture Rules*, you'll see we've expanded this list. As with all of our work over the years, we always reserve the right to get smarter. In the next section, we'll help you think specifically about critical gaps and toxins.

Close Critical Gaps

Assuming you want to apply the third rule, surely you would start with critical gaps. This is often harder to do than you might think. Sometimes, our most serious gaps are also our blind spots. We have encountered leaders who have lived with their gaps so long, they have become oblivious to them. One story should be sufficient to illustrate the point.

In a call with the senior leadership team at a school, they shared their aspiration as having three components: Academic Excellence, Service to Others, and Leadership. Because the call was intended to serve them, Mark began to transition to address the question of how the leaders were amplifying their aspiration. Before he finished his transition, one of the leaders said, "Let's not talk about leadership today."

"Sure. Why not?" Mark asked.

"We don't do anything with leadership," the leader said.

Confused, Mark asked, "What do you mean?"

"We don't talk about it, we don't teach it, we don't even have a point of view on the topic."

"Is it on your website? Probably on page one?" Mark asked.

"Yes. Yes, it is."

Mark said, "We don't have to talk about leadership today. However, you need to ask someone to take it off your website. Every day it remains erodes your credibility, influence, and leadership."

We'll not play out the rest of the conversation. However, this is the perfect example of a critical gap. When there is an obvious, often blatant, disregard for some or all of your aspiration, you have a critical gap.

> ┌─ **PRACTICE!** ─────────────────────────
> Have a candid conversation with your leaders—ask them
> to help you identify any critical gaps currently existing in
> your organization. You probably need to probe this topic
> with several individual contributors as well. If you sur-
> face any issues, begin taking steps immediately to attack
> the gap(s).

Eliminate Toxins

Toxins are patterns of unhealthy or unproductive behavior. Left
unchecked, they will metastasize and kill an organization. You
don't have to search long to find numerous examples where leaders failed to act decisively or, in some cases, failed to act at all. Consider how much hardship and trauma might have been avoided at
Theranos, Lehman Brothers, Enron, WeWork (pre-IPO), and IBM
in the early 1990s had their leaders done things differently. Leaders must be ever-vigilant for the early signs of these pathogens.
Here are a few for you to watch for:

- Apathy
- Paranoia
- Unhealthy competition
- Loss of procedural discipline

- Countercultures
- Self-deception
- Failure to listen
- Mistrust

If you see any of the above or a myriad of other toxins, you
must engage. Don't wait; initiate! The quicker you deal with these,
the quicker your organization can return to a healthy path toward
your aspiration.

┌─ **PRACTICE!** ─────────────────────────────────────┐

This is a two-part activity. First, brainstorm a list of a dozen additional *potential* toxins beyond the list above. Next, ask each member of your leadership team to rate all the toxins you've identified (plus the list above) on a 5-point scale: 1 = Nonexistent to 5 = Out of control. Do your initial assessment individually and then compare notes. Build your action plan based on what you learn.

└──┘

As we have tried to make the case for culture, we want to offer a friendly reminder: A healthy and vibrant culture is essential if you want to build a High Performance Organization, but it is *not* the goal. The goal is sustained levels of elite performance. There are two more moves your organization needs to make to reach the summit. Our encouragement to you is to stay the course—you'll be glad you did!

The ideas on the previous pages are a distillation of what we've learned over the years about the art and science of culture craft. If you'd like to do a deeper dive, read Culture Rules *or go to* **https://leadevery day.com/culture-rules**, *or scan this QR code:*

INCREASE ENGAGEMENT

The cost of disengagement is not just financial; it's cultural, and it's contagious.
—Jill Christensen

Have you ever worked on a team or in an organization where a high level of engagement was the norm? What did it feel like? How excited were you to go to work? Thankfully, we've worked in places like this. For us, the experience was life-giving, soul-enriching, and performance-enhancing. How does that description match your experience?

Let's flip the coin. Have you worked in an environment where engagement was low? What did it feel like? We're guessing it was the opposite of what we described above—it probably sucked the life out of you, crushed your soul, and hindered performance. Mark's dad told him stories of working in a place that had low engagement. He said some of his coworkers would knowingly ship defective parts just to fill an order, and it was maddening!

We can do better; you can do better. In the balance of this chapter, we'll explore four practices to help you increase the level of care your people feel and demonstrate at work. We will show you how to Increase Engagement.

Engagement has received a lot of press in leadership circles for the last 20 years or so. As if by some revelation, it was discovered that how much people care about their work, their coworkers, their customers, and their organization mattered. We think

215

this has always been the case and, frankly, will always be a relevant part of any conversation where sustained levels of elite performance is the ultimate goal. People who don't care don't consistently do great work—this doesn't feel like news to us. However, what may be newsworthy is the scope and scale of the issue. Engagement is a crisis of global proportions, a silent pandemic, and has been for years.

According to Gallup, the organization that brought engagement to the limelight, the total number of people fully engaged at work around the world has been hovering around 25% for more than a decade.[1] This explains much about the absence of truly great organizations. Just imagine trying to consistently produce world-class work if fewer than three in ten of your employees care. We would put this in the impossible category.

We can look at this global workforce malaise from several angles. First, we want to break with the pundits who interpret this data as a reflection of the sorry state of the workforce. We think engagement is a direct reflection of what leaders do or fail to do. Therefore, the dismal engagement numbers are an indictment of leadership. The second thing we'll say here is there may be no better time and opportunity for leaders and organizations to distinguish themselves. Because so few organizations have cracked the code on engagement, when you do, you will be uniquely positioned to lead your industry. You will have also created a place where people want to work and they'll stay longer—you'll have discovered your next competitive advantage.

One more thing: Although some think of engagement as "soft," according to Gallup, high engagement leads to *23% greater profitability*. Would you consider all that extra cash "soft?"[2]

Let's not get ahead of ourselves. This chapter is about engagement, not performance per se. We need a fully engaged workforce, but we can never forget, engagement is *not* the goal. No more than making more leaders and building a strong culture are. These things, along with engagement, are all enablers. You know where this is headed—we want to help you build a High Performance Organization. Each of these moves is critical if you are serious about achieving and sustaining elite levels of performance. Back to engagement—if you can't clear this hurdle, you are doomed to mere flashes of brilliance and the bitter, lingering taste of mediocrity.

NO HIRED HANDS

Have you ever heard the term *hired hands*? Have you thought about what the term implies? It's a term we think every organization in the world should ban. Maybe you don't use this language, but the spirit of it may still permeate your culture.

In the years between 1890 and 1930, the world changed. Prior to this time, large mass-production manufacturing and distribution companies didn't exist. This was the era when the modern corporation was born. In these growing organizations, leaders had no precedent for how to deal with the scope and scale they faced. Their response in part was structural—this is where departments, divisions, and middle managers were conceived. Although consequential for sure, the greatest invention of these newly formed organizations was wage labor. Wage labor had existed in agrarian settings for millennia, but this was different. Previously, it was common for the workers to bring knowledge, skills, and even their own tools to the job. All of this was about to change.

The growing market's demand created larger and larger organizations. In 1870, McCormick was one of the largest manufacturing facilities in America with only 500 employees. By 1900, more than 70 companies had more than 2,000 employees with dozens approaching 10,000. To find the needed labor, the companies increasingly turned to immigrants. One of their discoveries: The language barriers were real. To combat this, they began to simplify the tasks on the assembly line so communication would become less of an obstacle.[3]

Another hurdle leaders faced was absenteeism at rampant levels. In some cases, as many as 10% of workers were "missing" at the start of each day. The typical response was to go to the factory gate and find a replacement to staff the assembly line. This daily ritual fueled the urgency to get workers up to speed quickly; this also drove the need to further simplify the job—"all we need is their hands."

In 1911, a mechanical engineer named Frederick Taylor published the book *The Principles of Scientific Management*. Because the Second Industrial Revolution was gaining steam, organizations everywhere were interested in Taylor's new methods.

Before the turn of the century, work was largely controlled by the worker. In those days, unions were craft monopolies requiring five- to seven-year apprenticeships. Scientific management, however, changed all of this. Taylor put all the responsibility for getting work done on management. As some have summarized the heart of Taylorism, "Leaders think, supervisors talk, and workers work." This aligned perfectly with the practices that had already begun to take hold. Now, these practices were "validated" by Taylor's methods. The implications of his philosophy still haunt the world today.[4]

Taylor's ideas were so countercultural, Congress called a special hearing in 1911. The labor unions foreshadowed many of the problems we see in our modern workforce. They warned that workers solely employed for their hands would not bode well for the individuals, the organization, or our nation. Although we cannot find the words *disengaged workforce* in the official proceedings, that is how we can summarize their concerns. As it turned out, their warning was prophetic. More than a hundred years later, we can now say, with history as our guide, hired hands are not the panacea Taylor promised.[5]

In some ways, the stubbornness of our engagement metrics, as evidenced by their lack of improvement over the years, can be credited to the legacy of Taylor and the inability of many leaders to fight tendencies that have persisted now for more than a century. Our thinking has become stuck in the past. Even the modern backlash from leaders against remote work probably has roots in Taylor's beliefs. We think Taylor would quickly align with the sentiment that workers must be observed and closely supervised. We must re-elevate the way we think about the people we lead.

Although this dilemma has all the makings of conspiracy, it's more likely the by-product of overworked and ill-informed leaders doing the best they can. Some legacies die hard. In this next section, we'll try to put Taylorism to rest for good. "Workers" are capable of much more than we typically give them credit for—no hired hands!

CARE BEGETS CARE

Before we go any further, we need to pause and share our point of view on engagement. There is so much confusion in the world at large on the essence, meaning, and contours of this topic. As we've said previously, we believe a problem well-defined is half-solved. Regarding engagement, let's be clear on our definition.

Engagement in the workplace is a state of mind that directly reflects how much someone cares about their work, their coworkers, their customers, and their organization.

The leadership challenge, then, is simple: Create a place where people will care more.

What does it take to get workers to care more? Our guess is it's not what you may think as demonstrated by an odd cultural blip on the historical timeline of management and leadership practice. Many years from now, historians will be writing the history of leadership, and we're guessing they will include the contributions of Taylor, Drucker, and others. They will probably mention the intense focus on engagement that began around the turn of this century. We can also imagine a sidebar written on what we call the "Ping-Pong Experiment."

Some of you will remember the media coverage Google began to attract in the early 2000s. The world was fascinated with their culture and their employee engagement. In many of those news stories, one item was prominent . . . their Ping-Pong tables. Mark has visited the Google headquarters and, yes, he did see the tables with his own eyes. What followed all this media exposure was a mad dash by many organizations desperately wanting to improve their culture and engagement to purchase Ping-Pong tables.

If your organization purchased one of these tables in the last decade, thanks for trying! We're sure your heart was in the right place. When was the last time you played a game on that table? Unfortunately, creating culture and lifting engagement is far more complex than adding a game room at your headquarters.

If games at the office aren't the silver bullet, what is? If we want the people in our organization to care more, we must provide CARE—Connection, Affirmation, Responsibility, and the right Environment.

CREATE CONNECTION

Do you care about people, places, and things with which you have no connection? Probably not. This is the reason you've never rented a car and washed it before you returned it. As leaders, we need to help people connect in four critical areas.

The Work

Have you ever been in the wrong job? We hope not. But if you have, you know how it feels. If you've never had this experience, imagine what it would be like to invest your working hours doing something you didn't have the skill or competency to do or had no passion for; the word *drudgery* comes to mind.

Mark had an experience like this as a kid just out of high school. He worked at a local Chick-fil-A restaurant. He was not good at the work. As he tells the story decades removed, he confesses to still not being good with his hands. This created a slowness that is anathema in the fast-paced world of a quick-service restaurant. The tension grew until Mark made a strategic career decision—he quit. His rationale: It would be easier to explain his departure if he initiated it versus being fired. Mark found his way to Chick-fil-A's corporate headquarters and joined their team working in the warehouse and mail room—things worked out fine for him in the end.

Mark was not a good fit for the job—as a result, he was not connected to the organization in a meaningful way. How many of the people in your company are in the wrong role and yet stay on your payroll? This may be the worst possible scenario. We believe this is one of the contributing factors to the phenomenon of "quiet quitting." Help people find the right role on your team and the first connection point is secure.

If you are struggling to figure out your ideal job, Randy wrote a book entitled Finding Your Way. *Here's a link to learn more:* **https://lead everyday.com/finding-your-way**, *or scan this QR code:*

Coworkers

How do you foster and facilitate care and connection between your team members? This is perhaps where the Ping-Pong table could fit, if people actually used the tables. You help people connect with other humans when they spend time together and when they know each other on a personal level. Too many work relationships are just that—all about work. How can you help people know each other as humans, not just coworkers?

You may recall in the "Build Genuine Community" chapter we shared several ideas on how to help your team members know each other deeply. Build on these ideas.

Customers

Does every person in your organization understand who the customer is? For most roles, everyone has two customers: their internal customers and the ultimate customer, the one paying the bills. The further away from the ultimate customer an employee is, the more you'll need to amplify their voice.

One of Mark's colleagues and mentors at Chick-fil-A led the purchasing and distribution part of the enterprise for many years. In order to help his brand-new team members understand the importance of the customer, he didn't ask them to report to the headquarters on their first day on the job. Instead, he asked them to meet him at one of the chain's restaurants. He wanted them to meet the Operator and team members who were counting on them to provide the supplies they needed to serve their guests. He also wanted to spend time with the ultimate customer—those enjoying the product.

Use your imagination. There are many ways to help your entire organization stay connected to their customers. When they do, they will care more.

Organization

Why would people in your organization feel connected to it? What reasons have you given them? Do you have a compelling purpose? If you do, do people know it? Do you have a cause you are a champion for? Have you invited your team to join you?

SWIA is a long-standing client we mentioned in a previous chapter. They have chosen finding the cure for cystic fibrosis as one of the causes they support. The company hosts and sponsors events, matches employee contributions, and more. Over the years, they have raised over $3.5 million for their cause. Do you think the fact their employees feel connected to the organization makes a difference in their engagement and, ultimately, their performance? Absolutely. A caring organization attracts and retains people who care.

At the heart of any successful organization is its ability to genuinely care about people—both internally and externally. Genuine connection is often the key to fostering this kind of caring culture.

A few years ago, we had the opportunity to spend some time with Howard Behar, former president of Starbucks. During his tenure, the company grew from 17 locations to more than 20,000. We spoke specifically about the importance of connection in leadership. His advice was simple, straightforward, and action-able: "Have real conversations with people about your hopes and dreams for your organization. Putting words on the walls has some value, but nothing will ever replace the need for real conversations."[6]

```
┌─ PRACTICE! ──────────────────────────────────┐
│                                               │
│  This week, schedule a few conversations to talk with indi-  │
│  viduals in your organization. Work to connect with them  │
│  as a human being. Find out how connected they feel to the  │
│  organization's overall vision.               │
│                                               │
└───────────────────────────────────────────────┘
```

PROVIDE AFFIRMATION

The next strategy to increase the level of care (aka engagement) of your employees is to provide affirmation. This is a little tricky because so many people use the terms *recognition* and *affirmation* interchangeably, but they are not the same.

Recognition is easier, but less effective in driving engagement. We're still fans of recognition, and it has benefits beyond the scope of this section. We want you to raise the bar and think about how you can provide affirmation.

Affirmation is about really seeing someone and for them to feel seen. This requires extra time and energy on the part of leaders, but make no mistake, the dividends are huge.

Here's an activity you can try: Schedule one-on-one meetings with as many people under your leadership as possible. If you have thousands of employees, you can start with your inner cir-cle. Mark did this with an entire department once and talked to scores of people, including entry-level, individual contributors, and contractors. You can go as deep and wide as your calendar permits.

When you meet, there is only one question: What is the best recognition you've ever received? Now, note the question is about recognition; as we mentioned earlier, we want to set the bar higher. What you'll discover is that if people are willing to tell you about their *favorite* recognition, it is most likely their favorite because they found it most affirming. Be prepared for a wide array of responses. If you ask enough people, we're guessing you'll probably hear:

- A personal note
- A plaque or trophy
- Cash
- Public recognition

- Paid time off
- A trip
- A promotion
- More responsibility

Why such diversity in responses? To borrow a phrase, different people have different love languages. When you really know someone, you can speak in a way that honors them as an individual. This is why affirmation is more time-consuming and more powerful. Work hard to become fluent in the affirmation language of the people in your organization. When you really know people and see them as individuals, your leadership will improve—and they will care more.

PRACTICE!

Begin scheduling meetings to explore the various affirmation desires of your team members. We know you're busy—even if you have only one meeting a week, you will make progress.

SHARE RESPONSIBILITY

Do you remember the first big project assignment you were ever given? If that takes you too far back, think about your last big project. Think about how you felt when someone said, "We want you to own this," or, "Get this done—this is your responsibility." No doubt many thoughts probably rushed through your head and heart. Maybe some doubts: *Am I capable of doing this? What if I don't succeed?* Or, maybe a totally different set of responses: *What an opportunity!* Or, *I was born for this.* Our guess is most of us have had a mixture of thoughts and feelings in these situations—different emotions and reactions; a blend of optimism and apprehension would be normal. What is not up for debate is what happened to your level of care. When you were given real responsibility, you cared more—guaranteed.

Leaders are generally fairly good at delegating tasks, as they should be. A delegated task does transfer some sense of responsibility and will generate an uptick in the recipient's level of care as promised. However, if you want to raise the stakes and the level of care, try delegating outcomes and the decisions necessary to deliver those outcomes. This will generate the highest return in terms of engagement.

A final thought here for the sake of clarity. We are huge fans of accountability. But make no mistake—regardless of what a leader delegates, the leader is still ultimately accountable for the outcome.

┌─ PRACTICE! ─────────────────

Identify something you are currently investing your time on—a problem you are attempting to resolve or an opportunity you would like to seize—and decide who you might ask to take responsibility for this work.

OPTIMIZE THE ENVIRONMENT

In addition to the elements listed above, there are several other factors that will contribute greatly to a culture that produces people who care deeply.

Let's pull up and look at this situation from a higher altitude. You have been thinking about your organization a lot over the course of this book. How much thought have you given to the context in which people work?

The environment leaders create has tremendous impact on the engagement of the workforce. You ultimately control several key levers essential to the creation of a place where people and ideas can flourish. This is what happened about 800 years ago, during the Renaissance.[7]

As a refresher for those who may have forgotten a few of the details, the Renaissance was a period between the Middle Ages and the modern era, generally agreed to be between AD 1350 and 1600.[8]

The word *Renaissance* means "rebirth"—a new way to think and see the world. A fresh wind began to blow in Florence and eventually spread throughout Europe. Art, science, literature, astronomy, exploration, philosophy, and religion were reborn during this period. Even learning and communication were impacted with the invention of movable type. Virtually no facet of life was left untouched by this period of history. The Renaissance brought new life and vitality to every corner of Europe, and its impact is still felt today.

How does something like this happen? While scholars have debated this question for centuries, we have our own theory.

The defining characteristic of the era was passion. What is passion? Nothing more than extreme levels of care.

Consider Galileo, whose views landed him under house arrest

for the last 11 years of his life, yet he wouldn't recant. Or Martin Luther, whose beliefs caused him to be excommunicated from the church. There were many others who, without their passion and conviction, would not have changed the world. Why did these people care so much? That is *the* question.

As we've already outlined in the previous pages, there was not a *single* causal factor. There were many elements that converged to create this cultural phenomenon—a combination of the right people, high levels of interaction and collaboration, physical proximity, and resources. If you're wondering about what type of resources, it was primarily money. Wealthy families like the Medicis were very generous commissioning works by many artists. However, resources were also provided by countless others. Even the church got in on the action; that's why Michelangelo agreed to paint the ceiling of the Sistine Chapel—Pope Julius II was a well-funded and persuasive client.

Finally, the mindset of the people was an essential part of the context. Coming out of decades of famine and disease sometimes appropriately called the Dark Ages, there was an openness to new thinking, a spirit of innovation, a willingness to try new things and challenge existing conventions. It was a wonderful dynamic. This renaissance mindset ultimately swept the region and then the continent.

For a modern example of creating an environment to stimulate enhanced levels of engagement and innovation, Mark recalls a time when he was searching for ideas for a space he was designing at the company's headquarters for his team.

The Chick-fil-A headquarters built in 1982 was an award-winning design—a 1980s design. Decades later, Mark was trying to create a space to foster creativity, collaboration, and innovation. None of these were design parameters in the previous build. One of his visits took him to Pixar. He recalls being amazed at the level of thinking the leaders put into constructing a place where the employees were charged with creating memories and moments of wonder for the entire world.

The teams had both common space and individual space—a nod to the fact that creative work demands both team time and alone time. All the amenities—the cafeteria, the post office (yes, they had a post office), the store with all the swag, and more—were centrally located in a large atrium so people from the far reaches of the building would converge and commingle on a regular basis. Pixar capitalized on many of the lessons of the Renaissance—they created a purpose-built environment.

Let's go back to our example of the Renaissance and see what we can transfer across time and space to the organizations we lead. The environmental factors at play that helped create an era of highly engaged and passionate people included:

Proximity & Collaboration

Putting talented and passionate people together in close proximity appears to create positive outcomes. Here are a few examples from the period.

Many of the creators who are well known today studied together in the same studio. One of the more famous examples is Andrea del Verrocchio's workshop: Leonardo da Vinci, Botticelli, and Pietro Perugino all trained there.[9]

Leonardo da Vinci and Michelangelo were commissioned to paint battle scenes on opposite walls of the Palazzo Vecchio in Florence (1504–1506). This direct competition became known as the "Battle of the Frescoes."[10]

Both Michelangelo and Raphael worked in the Vatican at the same time (c. 1508–1512).

While Michelangelo was painting the Sistine Chapel ceiling, Raphael decorated the papal apartments.

Perugino and Michelangelo competed for the commission to paint the Sistine Chapel ceiling—as we all know, this was a contest Michelangelo ultimately won.[11]

Despite all the trends toward remote work, we are not sure the Renaissance could have happened over Zoom. Talented people in close proximity helped accelerate the movement of ideas and innovation. This practice still works today.

Resources

In our Renaissance example, this was primarily money gladly offered by the wealthy benefactors of the day. Financial resources still matter. Do the people in your organization have enough money to do what they've been asked to do?

What other environmental factors must leaders pay attention to? There are a few more things to consider to create the perfect storm of care and engagement.

Skills

If you want to demonstrate care for the people in your organization, be sure they have the skills required to do the job. Often, we can assume people possess the needed skills when they don't. If the skills don't align with the assignment, engagement will never go up—it will go down. The only passion you'll see from those who lack the skills is a passion to leave your organization.

Safety

When we think about safety, we believe most people think about physical safety. Clearly, this should be a nonnegotiable. However, there is another facet to the question of safety. If left unchecked, this one can thwart all your engagement efforts—psychological safety. People who don't feel safe emotionally are never going to care as much as you need them to.

- Do people in your organization feel comfortable voicing their opinions?
- Are you open to new and different perspectives?
- Are contrarian views welcomed?
- What are you doing subconsciously to create an unsafe environment?

You may be wondering which came first, the elements that combined to create the Renaissance or the mindset? The interplay between the people and the elements, driven by the mindset, enabled the Renaissance to create its own energy. The same will be true in your organization. If we want people to care deeply, like the artists, thinkers, craftsmen, theologians, and musicians of the Renaissance, leaders must create the right environment.

PRACTICE!

Do an audit of your workplace environment. Which of the elements mentioned above is in short supply? Take action, or at least begin the planning, to address the shortfall.

HONOR, DIGNITY, AND RESPECT

As you consider the engagement of those on your team or in your organization, we challenge you to own this. We've talked to leaders who are unwilling to do so. In these situations, the employee is left to figure things out on their own. This rarely works. The fundamental problem with this approach is that the essential elements required to create high levels of engagement are not within the control of most employees. These men and women depend on the organization to provide the raw ingredients:

Connection
Affirmation
Responsibility
Environment

When leaders provide care in this form, the people in your organization will care more. We know there are skeptics among you, and that's okay. We appeal to your better angels to give this a try.

If you will think about engagement a bit differently, we believe your reality will change. Rather than think about engagement as something you *have* to focus on and a burden you must carry, consider this new paradigm: What would happen if your goal was to treat every employee with honor, dignity, and respect? How might you accomplish this? You could start by increasing your level of CARE.

FOCUS ON EXECUTION

When it absolutely, positively, has to be there overnight.
—Federal Express, 1978

What is execution worth—really? This section has focused on how to Strengthen Your Organization and we've covered three of the four moves every High Performance Organization makes: Develop More Leaders, Build the Culture, and Increase Engagement. This chapter, "Focus on Execution," is the final move.

We believe we know what some of you are thinking. There may even be a group who skipped directly to this chapter. If so, no judgment! Leaders care about execution. We are paid to help our organizations produce results and we know from experience that the better we execute, the better the results.

A leader who heard our four moves for the first time exclaimed, "Now you're talking!" when we mentioned execution. He said, "I don't care about all that other crap. We're just going to *execute*." He put a little extra energy and emphasis on the word that mattered so much to him.

Again, we get it. Any leader worth anything wants to execute. However, consider the gymnast who says, "I just want to do the dismount." Where do they get the height, energy, and momentum to stick the landing? All of this comes from the routine that precedes the dismount.

Execution is much like the dismount in gymnastics. When

we watch the Olympics from our homes, we will never see many of the deductions the judges see in the routines, but we will all see the dismount. It's the same with our customers. They may not understand the intricacies of our process but they all see the dismount, the product or service you sold them. Was it on time? Was it defect-free? Does it do what you said it would? These questions are inescapable.

This is why, as critical as the previous moves (and chapters) are, none of them are the goal. Execution and the performance consistent execution enables are the ultimate prize.

Everything you do should ultimately contribute to higher levels of execution.

HOW GOOD DO YOU WANT TO BE?

How good is your organization when it comes to execution? Look at the numbers. Someone in your organization has them. What's your defect or error rate? How many dissatisfied customers do you have in a month or year? At least, how many do you know about? You may want to look at the number of late deliveries or your client retention rate. If you don't know the answers to these questions or others like them, you probably need to search them out. Why? Greatness hinges on execution!

Here's our challenge to you—you have a fundamental question to answer: How good do you want to be? Every organization answers this question. Some would say, "We want to be world-class." Really? Are you producing world-class results? Others would take what appears to be a more pragmatic and short-term view: "We want to be better than our competition." This might work for a season. Maybe this is easy because, currently, your competition is mediocre at best. Do you really want your competitive advantage to be, "We're the best of a bad lot"? We believe you can do better than "We're not awful—do business with us!"

If any of these comments hits a little close to home, you need to be aware of a few inherent risks. One, what happens if one of your competitors decides to get a lot better? What will you do then? Two, what if a new competitor enters your industry? Or three, with value widely held as what you get for what you pay, if your product or service is not reliably excellent, what happens if a competitor significantly lowers their prices?

Maybe you think you're good enough. We've met leaders who are thrilled if their error rate stays below 10%. Their logic is that 90% is still an "A." Maybe in algebra, but in today's competitive landscape, this is a very slippery slope.

Try this: Take your current error, defect, or return rate and calculate how many *people* your performance impacts. We are advocates of reporting these types of numbers as people versus percentage. Randy talked to a leader whose *goal* was 95% accuracy. On the surface, 95% sounds really good. However, try converting this percentage to *people*. This business served over 3,000 people per day, six days a week. Here's the math: 3,000 customers x .05% error rate = 150 customers a day with a problem. Now, multiply this by six days a week = 900 customers a week with a problem. Now, the last step. Multiply this by 52 weeks = 46,800 customers (about twice the seating capacity of Madison Square Garden) with an issue. You probably don't want to set a *goal* to mess up almost 50,000 customer orders in a single year.

We hope your reaction is the same as most leaders: "Well, 95% doesn't sound as good when you say it like that." You are correct. Unfortunately, saying it this way reflects the brutal facts.

Brace yourself. We recommend an execution *goal* of 100%. We say it like this:

The goal is to do the right thing, the right way, every time.

Now, before you stop reading and throw this book in the trash, please read the next paragraph very carefully.

We know this goal is impossible. However, it is the goal, *not* an expectation. There is an enormous difference between the two. An unachievable expectation creates anxiety, stress, fear, and frustration. However, a challenging goal, properly positioned, can lead to strong motivation. How much lower do you want to set your sights? How many customers do you *want* to jeopardize?

If you are willing to set this audacious goal, it will impact your mindset. In turn, your mindset will impact your behavior, and ultimately, your behavior will determine your outcomes.

WHERE DO WE BEGIN?

When we set our minds on learning how the best organizations in the world executed at such an elevated level, our first step was to call our friends at Stanford and ask them to do a literature review. We've taken this approach before, but their response was different this time. They said they would need six months. We were astonished at the lengthy timeline but commissioned the work nonetheless. As the deadline approached, we received a call requesting time for them to share what they had learned. They asked for a *full day* to make their presentation. Honestly, this felt a bit excessive, but we said yes. We're thankful we granted their request. The summary of their work resulted in a deck of 200 slides! As it turns out, the world knows a lot about execution.

We have a bias toward the simple while remaining ever vigilant not to drift into the simplistic. We knew what we learned that day was certainly true, but there was a lot of work for us to do. We entered what we called the *translation stage* of our work. Our charge: How do we make the truth about this topic approachable, applicable, and actionable?

Thankfully, we were able to discover a simple approach to help any organization improve its execution. In the balance of this chapter, we'll do a couple of things: We'll share the three big ideas that will transform your organization and your execution, and we'll talk about a best practice for each that will leverage the time and influence of your leaders.

We'll begin with the big insight that drove everything that follows. With most of our work over the last 25 years, we have focused almost exclusively on leadership behavior. In this case, we quickly realized that would be the wrong path. If your organization wants to accomplish extraordinary things in the realm of execution, you have to accept one simple truth: *The magic is in the masses.*

Elite levels of execution are only possible to the extent in which you enroll every member of your organization. How many employees do you have in your organization? Write down a number in the margin of the book. Do it now. If you don't know, estimate.

Let's say you have 100 employees. Here's how you become the best in your industry at execution: Get all 100 people in your organization to do the following three things.

- Pursue Mastery
- Own the Numbers
- Help Others Win

PURSUE MASTERY

Execution cannot be mandated or coerced over a long period of time. You can build incentives, challenge and celebrate people, and even punish those who fail to hit your standards. But when things get tough, and they always do, the motivation to do the right thing, the right way, every time must come from deep within every individual on your team. This first step requires *everyone* to make a personal commitment to learn, grow, and improve every day—to pursue mastery.

Mastery is a level of skill in which three things are true: The desired behavior is consistent, the execution is flawless, and the behavior becomes second nature.

Remember our comments earlier about a goal versus an expectation? This message was underscored when our research took us to meet with some of the coaches from Clemson University. At the time, they were one of the best collegiate football programs in America. We showed up in the middle of their impressive National Championship streak, when they played for the championship four times in eight years, with victories in 2016 and 2018. We learned their coaches didn't expect a player to execute their assignment flawlessly on every play. We know that sounds crazy at some level. The coaches would say to the player, "We want you to embrace the *goal* to make every block correctly, and we're going to coach you to help you continue to improve your success rate."

Viktor Frankl said, "Between stimulus and response there is a space. In that space is our power to choose our response. In our response lies our growth and our freedom."[1] When a player or an employee decides they are willing to leverage this thin space and choose the path of mastery, everything changes for the good.

How do you enroll your employees to Pursue Mastery? That's a big question! You'll want to begin with selection. Some people love the idea of mastery, while for others it sounds like a lot of work—which it is. For people already on your team, you will need to cast a compelling vision for why Pursuing Mastery is a life skill, not just a work thing. Men and women who set exacting standards for themselves will have few regrets. You'll also want to celebrate those who join you on the journey. Honor those who are with you by your example. Remember, people always watch the leader.

Coach for Life

This best practice may seem counterintuitive. We're talking about how to Excel at Execution at work, so why would we suggest leaders Coach for Life? Because we're leading people—human beings who have a life beyond work. Some will be surprised we included this as a result of our research. We will say it wasn't universally present. However, for those leaders who took a more holistic view of their role and the lives of the people they led, the results were impressive.

Many leaders have found tremendous value in spending time with individual employees. During these one-on-one sessions, a listening leader can discover a person's hopes, dreams, aspirations, and challenges at work. If people are willing to share, a leader could learn what's going on in someone's life outside of work. Conversations like this do several things. They increase connections, a key factor in engagement. If you have conversations like this, they will help you lead an individual better. Your demonstration of care will foster trust in you, and by extension, the organization. Finally, if you have these interactions, the chances of these people accepting your challenge to Pursue Mastery increase significantly. Maybe for the first time, the individual believes you care about them beyond what they can do for you and the organization. We've seen few (if any) examples in which "cogs in the corporate machine" are willing to Pursue Mastery. You can acknowledge the value and merit of the whole person.

┌─ PRACTICE! ─────────────────────────────────

Begin scheduling dream conversations with your team members. If you would like, you can combine this **Practice!** activity with the one on page 225 regarding affirmation.

OWN THE NUMBERS

On a cold January night, we took 163 leaders bowling. There was a low level of excitement as we drove across town—it had been a long day and a half. The attendees had been sequestered in a hotel ballroom learning the ins and outs of elite levels of execution. This was going to be a much-needed break.

When we arrived, the group was told we had rented the entire venue. All they needed to do was choose their shoes, ball, and a lane. We would start as soon as everyone was in place. As the participants began to move into the facility, if you were paying attention, you could sense something wasn't right. Murmuring was heard among the group. At first, only a few noticed, and then a few more; there was something different about this bowling alley—there were no pins!

Well, maybe there were pins, but they couldn't be sure. All the pins were hidden behind curtains. Yes, our team had arrived hours earlier and covered all the pins. We were about to engage in what someone called Blind Bowling.

The protests began immediately. "We can't bowl. We can't see the pins. Why would we waste our time if we can't see the pins? This is crazy!" Our response was, "Your job is to bowl. Roll the ball."

What happened next was ridiculous. As people rolled the ball time and time again, some would listen intently to try and discern how many pins they had toppled. "I think I got nine," someone might say in an excited tone, and one of their lane mates would respond, "I think you got two."

The outcry, along with the frustration, grew for about 45 minutes. For fear of our lives at that point, we gave the group a much-deserved break with food and free arcade access. While they were away, we removed the curtains so the pins were visible.

When they returned, their response was interesting. We told them they could resume their bowling. They loved it! Odd. It was the same ball, the same smelly shoes, and the same little fan to dry their hands. What changed? Well, that's obvious. They could see the pins and keep score. By the way, we didn't tell them how to keep score, and we had the electronic scoring turned off. In some groups, someone knew how to keep score. In groups where no one knew how, they googled it with no prompting from us to do so. They wanted to keep score.

After round two, another 45 minutes, we told them they needed to stop, which many of them didn't want to do. Our debrief was simple: only a few questions.

"How was round one?" The consensus was—*awful*! The language used to describe those first 45 minutes was colorful and detailed. You can use your imagination.

"How was round two?" *Fantastic, fun, enjoyable.*

"Why?"

"We could see the pins and keep score."

"Final question: How was your round one experience different from what your employees are feeling if they have never seen the pins?"

Here's the truth: Too many people are Blind Bowling at work. Without measurement, their engagement is low and they never do their best work. As a result, achieving elite levels of execution is impossible. Measurement drives improvement. As leaders, we need to help people know and Own the Numbers. By *own*, we mean accepting responsibility for their numbers and working to improve them. If you want to become a better bowler, you need to see the pins. If you want to improve your execution, the same is true.

Find the Number

The previous story illustrates several things:

1. People love to keep score.
2. People who don't know the score quickly become disinterested or disengaged.
3. You can't keep score without knowing the numbers.

One of the easiest ways to improve execution is to be sure everyone has at least one number they can track. In an ideal world, it will be a number they can personally impact. What could you track daily (maybe even hourly)? Try to avoid a number that is published only once a month, such as profitability. Yes, you want everyone to care about profits, but what are the factors that directly contribute to profits? In a restaurant, for example, someone working in the kitchen could track waste—less waste equals more profits. Extraordinary things happen when every role has a goal.

```
┌─ PRACTICE! ──────────────────────────────────────┐
│                                                   │
│  Work to establish at least one number that matters, or │
│  should matter, for each employee. Figure out how to help │
│  them track this number.                          │
│                                                   │
└───────────────────────────────────────────────────┘
```

Focus on Process

Once your team Owns the Numbers, you can add tremendous value by helping people focus on the process. We've said this before—your current systems, processes, beliefs, and behaviors are perfectly aligned with the results you are now receiving. If you want to help people improve their numbers and the organization's key metrics, ensure that people are following the existing processes. If they are, and the numbers aren't improving, work to improve the process. Process makes excellence repeatable.

Work to isolate the root cause of the greatest contributor to your execution challenges. Maybe you'll learn that a specific shift struggles more than others, or the origin of your issue appears to be linked to a particular product. Maybe there is a single team leader who is linked to the problem. Outline the process. If the problem can be traced to a specific product or service, ask yourself if there is an issue with the raw ingredients. The assembly? The packaging? How were the people preparing or manufacturing this product trained? Do a full-blown problem-solving exercise. Don't jump to a conclusion. As an example, if a shift leader is not meeting the expectations for their role, ask yourself why not. Was it a selection issue? Was it a training issue? Is there an opportunity to improve communications? Where did the process break down?

┌─ **PRACTICE!** ─────────────────────────────

Pick one outcome or key result area in need of improvement. Do a full assessment of the process using the ideas
above. Work to shift the conversation from what is not
right to why it's not right. Focus on the process, not the
people. Your goal is to first identify potential root causes
and ultimately make the necessary changes to the process
to ensure the desired outcome(s).

───

HELP OTHERS WIN

One of the more surprising findings from the team's research was
the power of a shared effort. This shouldn't have surprised us after
decades of work building High Performance Teams. Perhaps it was
the magnitude of the impact that caught us off guard.

In 30 pilot groups, we introduced the idea of helping those
on your team win in the context of execution. We encouraged
participants to coach, train, celebrate, correct, and assist their
teammates in any way they could to improve the organization's
execution. Remember, we had already asked the people to commit
to Pursuing Mastery and Owning the Numbers. This would be the
final piece of the puzzle.

To help facilitate this third big idea, we deployed an app with
a few simple questions the team members would answer at the
end of each shift. The question that captured everyone's attention
was simply this:

How did you help someone win today?

In 3 months, testing the concept in only 30 locations, we had
almost 40,000 responses to this question—over 20 per participant!

The amount of energy around this idea of Help Others Win

was astonishing. Giving people permission to serve others, who they knew had made the same commitment to Pursue Mastery, unleashed a power most of the participants had never experienced. They engaged at an entirely new level.

While visiting one of the pilot locations, Mark encountered a young woman who was extremely excited about the execution project. She said it had transformed the way she viewed work and added, "Now, when I walk in the door, I'm looking for ways to Help Others Win."

Mark asked, "Why?"

She said, "Have you heard about our app? I don't want to get to the end of my shift and not have an answer to the question."

The impact of encouraging people to Help Others Win touched more than the frontline team members. Leaders expressed disbelief and some concern. They weren't sure this was a good idea. Historically, their role had focused on coaching, training, correcting, celebrating, and assisting the team. Now, everyone had been deputized. Some leaders asked us, "Is it okay that everyone is helping me do my job?" Others, quite sheepishly, admitted their job was now significantly easier.

You're probably anxious to hear the results. In some cases, they were brilliant and beyond our wildest imagination. However, intellectual integrity demands that we admit the shortcomings of our pilot group. Many did not see the results any of us had hoped for. Some couldn't even implement the activities we suggested.

As we have stated repeatedly, the ultimate goal is elite levels of performance *sustained* over time. To do this requires *all four* moves. Those who struggled with executing consistently were just not ready. The leaders in our partner organizations had not invested enough time and energy on developing more leaders, building their cultures, and increasing engagement.

If people are not well-led, they are not aligned, their engagement is lacking, you cannot Excel at Execution—our pilot validated what in retrospect feels like common sense.

Communicate Tirelessly

One of the best practices that gave life to this work was communication. Communication is the oxygen of execution. However, for this to be true, the focus of the messaging does need to be execution. One of our pilot locations significantly ramped up communications with no real impact on their execution. Further investigation revealed their increased efforts were focused on the people—birthdays, anniversaries, and so on. This was probably great for the culture but really didn't move the key execution metrics.

Over the years, we've seen scores of ways leaders have effectively communicated the critical message of execution. Here are a few that have made a significant difference.

Team Huddles. This may be the most challenging and perhaps the most effective way we've seen leaders keep the Focus on Execution on a daily basis. This is not a new idea. Horst Schulze, the former head of the Ritz-Carlton Hotel Company, told us years ago, your organization will never realize its full potential until you master team huddles (the implication was that this was true for all organizations).

Huddles can keep your people focused daily on what matters and why. The best team huddles we've seen are short, five to seven minutes; they are preplanned with predetermined key talking points; and they reinforce cultural messages and keep the Focus on Execution. Randy had a season where his leadership team huddled every morning for three to five minutes to calibrate on what needed to be executed for the day. Their level of focus led to extraordinary growth in the organization. In our experience, the best team huddles translate to the best improvement in execution.

Interviews. Not everyone will want to be part of an organization committed to world-class levels of execution. How do you know? The best predictor of future behavior is past behavior. Be sure your interview process probes this person's past experience with execution. Is the concept new to them? How do they react? Were they on time for their interview? Was their application complete? If a person is not interested in Pursuing Mastery, Owning the Numbers, and Helping Others Win, find this out in the interview process. We believe everyone can be successful at work. However, not everyone can be successful in a High Performance Organization. What you are trying to create is rare and extremely valuable. You'll need the right people in every position to make your journey as friction free as possible. Learn as much as you can in the interview process. You'll save yourself frustration later.

Team Meetings. Team meetings come in all shapes and sizes. Whether an "all-hands" meeting or a leadership team meeting, keep execution on the agenda. If the idea of taking your execution to the next level is a totally new concept, you may want to call a meeting with everyone to cast the vision and set the expectations. Few people have ever seriously considered a definition of execution that includes: Do the right thing, the right way, every time. Also, many leaders have gone so far as to include the three big ideas in everyone's job description. If you want to go down this path, people will need to hear the vision and understand the strategy (Pursue Mastery, Own the Numbers, and Help Others Win). And they'll need to understand the initial implications for them. We are 100% sure there will also be questions.

Find numerous ways to increase your focused communication regarding execution. We'll repeat ourselves—communication is the oxygen of execution.

PRACTICE!

Ask someone to design a multifaceted communication plan to ensure that no one in your organization ever forgets the priority of doing the right thing, the right way, every time. If you are still looking for a project to fulfill the earlier **Practice!** challenge to share ownership, this might be a good option.

If you want a free PDF on a launch strategy to help your organization Win Every Day, go to ***https://leadeveryday.com/execution****, or scan this QR code:*

Will all this time and energy focused on execution be worth the effort? Only you can decide. However, your customers pay you to do something—deliver something, build something, service something. The doing is execution. Will your customers tolerate a few late deliveries or mistakes? Sure, for a while.

Value is ultimately calculated in the mind of every customer with a simple equation: What you get divided by what you pay equals perceived value—value is always subjective and determined by the buyer.

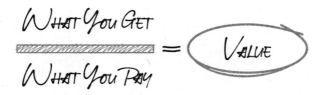

If a pattern develops in which the customer pays more than they receive in perceived value, chances are strong you'll lose a customer.

Sometimes, the stakes of execution are even higher than a single customer. Consider the example of an unnamed restaurant that had extremely low food safety scores. When you mess with food safety, you run the risk of doing far more than losing a customer. People can get sick and even die if standards aren't maintained. And think about the ripple effect on a brand should something go horribly wrong in an individual location. The leader and team in this case decided to embrace the disciplines from this chapter—Pursue Mastery, Own the Numbers, and Help Others Win. They executed the plan we've just outlined for you.

You guessed it—they saw unprecedented improvement. Now, for seven consecutive quarters, they have received the highest possible food safety ratings. Yes, not only is execution important; elite levels of execution are also achievable!

JUST MAKING OMELETS?

On a warm spring morning, for the third day in a row, Randy had just polished off one of the best omelets he had ever eaten. He was in Bradenton, Florida, at Pirate City, enjoying a spring training breakfast with the Pittsburgh Pirates' minor leaguers. The omelet maker was mesmerizing as he served player after player. Randy had never seen anything like it. The cook had 10 hot plates going at one time. Big professional athletes were filled with anticipation as they lined up for the first meal of the day.

The omelet maker, Ronald, looked up and said, "You're the egg white guy, correct?" Randy was thinking, *How does this guy even remember who I am, much less what I ordered the last two mornings?* There were more than 150 men in the camp. Although Randy was there to encourage and equip the coaches, he thought he would take a minute to encourage Ronald.

Randy said, "You're amazing at what you do."

"All in a day's work," Ronald replied.

"Seriously, you are making some incredible omelets here."

Ronald gave an unassuming, "Thanks."

"Don't you wish you knew how many omelets you've made?"

Ronald looked at Randy with stern eyes and said, "I do know how many I've made. Yesterday, I made one hundred twenty-six."

An hour later, Randy was with the big-league guys having a conversation with their manager at the time, Clint Hurdle.

"Do you know anything about Ronald, over at the minor-league facility?" Randy asked.

"I think I know that guy—what's up with him?"

Randy explained how Ronald was totally locked in, maybe more than many of the players in the camp.

"Why do you say that?" Clint asked.

Randy told Clint the whole story, the quality of the food, the fact that Ronald remembered his order, and was keeping his own scorecard!

"That doesn't surprise me," Clint said.

"Why not?"

"Because he's not just making omelets."

"What? I think he is. He just made three of the best ones I've had in my life."

"No, you don't understand. He's not *just* making omelets," Clint said.

"Well, then, what's he doing?" Randy asked, obviously confused.

"He's trying to win the World Series. We all are. Everyone in the organization, from ticket takers to stadium workers, to our MVP outfielder, and all the other players and coaches to the minor-league omelet maker. We all have one goal. We're trying to bring a championship to Pittsburgh."

In a beautiful moment of clarity, Clint reminded Randy that High Performance Organizations are well-led, aligned, engaged, and focused on execution. This is exactly what Randy had been training the coaching staff to do. The team was actually applying our content. That kind of focus comes only from leadership.

We have an aspiration for you and your organization. We dream of a day when no one in your organization is *just* making omelets, or *just* building widgets, or *just* taking customer calls, or *just* repairing leaking pipes, or "just" doing anything. We believe you can create an organization where people are pulling with you, against your competition and toward your goals. We are confident you can build a High Performance Organization.

As we close this chapter, we want to go back to the setup for this last section, Strengthen Your Organization. Please don't miss any of the moves. It is so easy for us to be captivated by the dismount. We all love to execute! We know the excitement of ever-improving performance. We understand the passion and energy your picture of the future stirs in your heart. All of this is within your reach *if* you Develop More Leaders, Build the Culture, and Increase Engagement. Then, and only then, can your organization's Focus on Execution consistently produce the results you desire.

Think of these four moves as the box top for the puzzle you are trying to put together. If you are missing a piece, your masterpiece will forever be incomplete, and you'll always wonder what might have been. Don't run the risk and live with regret. You and your team are capable of so much more than you know. When you build an organization capable of elite levels of performance sustained over time, a true High Performance Organization, the real fun has just begun.

Enjoy the journey!

EPILOGUE:
LEAD EVERY DAY

It does not matter how slowly you go as long as you do not stop.
—Confucius

Lee Gravitt, Randy's dad, had a long and successful career at Georgia Power Company. He started there as a 20-year-old kid in 1960 as a helper in the line crew. When Randy asked his dad what a helper in the line crew did, Lee's answer was simple—anything the line crew didn't want to do. Lee reminisced, "I was mostly digging holes for power poles, with no access to an auger." Have you ever used post hole diggers? They are brutal. "All the work was done by hand, but I was so excited; who wouldn't be? They paid me $1.67 per hour as opposed to the $1.04 I earned in my previous job working in a carpet mill! It was like hitting the lottery." Remember, this was 1960.

When Lee retired in 1995 with 35 years of service, he had held many different roles and moved into leadership along the way, finishing as the Area Manager for all of Northwest Georgia. He built an amazing legacy within the organization; they even named a substation after him that still bears his name some 30 years later.

Randy was at the retirement party and substation dedication for his dad. It was truly a wonderful day. There were little lemon cookies, a bowl full of punch with white foam on top, speeches from longtime teammates, lots of laughter, and even a few tears. Having family and friends there made the moment even more unforgettable.

As Randy processed all he experienced that day, he realized his dad's legacy wasn't built on that first day of hard labor or the last day of celebration—it was formed over the decades, in the everyday moments when he showed up, led by example, and made a difference. Whether it was under the hot Georgia sun, in the middle of the night, or on a rare frigid and icy morning, his dad and crews would show up and make sure people had their electricity so they could continue living in peace. Lee made one decision over and over again—he would Lead Every Day. This might challenge your instincts, but it's the truth.

Just like Randy's dad on his first day at Georgia Power, we all love beginnings. Whether it's starting a new relationship, the first day of school as a kid, a new job or fresh assignment, beginning a hobby, the arrival of summer, or the opening day of a sports season when your team is still undefeated—few things are as exciting as a good start. Yes, we love beginnings.

But let's be honest—there's also something about a great ending that captures us just as much. Think about the thrill of the *last* day of school, the final scene of an epic movie, graduation day, finishing a project, or reaching a goal. There's a special kind of satisfaction in crossing the finish line—like the rush someone feels when they complete a marathon and receive their medal. Good endings are unforgettable.

However, here's the truth: Your legacy isn't defined by the beginning or the end of your career. The real secret? It's what you do in between.

But who's excited about the middle? We typically hate the middle. We trudge through the middle of the day, complain about a midlife crisis, look back with horror on middle school, and hit the proverbial wall in the middle of a marathon. But middles matter more than we recognize.

Perhaps many of you are just beginning your career and you're in your first opportunity to lead, and the excitement is palpable. Others of you are probably nearing the end of your leadership journey, with retirement on the horizon, and you can already taste the lemon cookies. Truthfully, the two of us are much closer to the end than the beginning. But we are guessing most of you are somewhere in the middle.

We hope people will say nice things about you on your last day, but that day is not what will define you or your legacy. The words of affirmation matter, and they will be appreciated. They were an essential part of Randy's dad ending well, but oh, how middles are underrated.

Leaders are built, teams served, organizations strengthened, people cared for, and legacies built in the mundane middle. If you've been leading for any length of time, you know this. The long days, the hard days, the day your program was terminated... or you were! The time your budget was cut or the legal department said you couldn't do what needed to be done. The day your best employee and your heir apparent left to join the competition. The day the competition undercut your prices, and you lost 20% of your clients. There's another thing that can make the middle so agonizing: Many of the programs you initiate won't bear fruit for years; in some cases, decades. Leaders and legacies are forged in the crucible of time.

We also have to mention the facets of our legacy that have nothing to do with work—friendships, causes we support, family we cherish, the gift of our presence at ball games and ballet recitals, the weddings, the funerals we attend, and so much more. Here's the thing—those all occur in the mundane middle also. The life we want to create for ourselves and those who matter to us is not off somewhere in the future; it is now. Not at the beginning and not at the end. Stay the course, do the right things for the right reasons, and enjoy the journey. The prizes, and there are many, are found along the way in the pursuit, not at the finish line.

Why would we choose to close this book with this message? The answer is simple: The best leaders Confront Reality. And your reality is that you chose a hard profession. However, we don't want you to miss the innumerable rewards. We have the unbelievable opportunity to serve people and help them accomplish more than they ever thought possible. We can steward our talents and gifts in an organization we believe in. As leaders, we can literally invent the future and change our world. What's better than that?!

What is the key to unlocking all these benefits and more? Like Lee, we must embrace the mundane middle and Lead Every Day. That's where legacies are built, and the differences we make in our lives will surpass our wildest imaginations.

WHAT'S NEXT FOR YOU?

In a previous chapter, we posed a question that we want to ask you one more time. What are you and your team capable of? As we've already said, we don't know the specifics of your situation, but we do know this:

You are capable of much more than you can possibly imagine.

When you upload your new Operating System and embark on a lifelong journey to pursue three essential disciplines—Become a Better Leader, Improve Team Performance, and Strengthen Your Organization—you will unleash the passion and the performance of everyone around you.

Lead Every Day!

ACKNOWLEDGMENTS

From Mark:

As I've said before, this is my favorite part of the writing process. To have a moment to acknowledge some of the team that made the work possible is a treat.

This book is a distillation of almost all the work I've been part of for the last 25 years. As such, when challenged to write this section, I was reminded of the hundreds of people who brought the principles and practices out of the shadows so you and I could use them to change our world. To all of you, thank you!

What I'm about to do is very risky ... I'm going to call out *some* of the men and women who helped make this book possible.

Chick-fil-A Leadership—The Executive Committee, past and present, specifically CFA's former CEO Dan Cathy and the company's former presidents, both Tim Tassopoulos and Jimmy Collins, were instrumental in the creation of this content. To all of you, thank you! The world is better because of your leadership.

Chick-fil-A Operators—As mentioned in chapter 1, these independent business owners are amazing leaders. The ideas you've just read weren't created by Chick-fil-A but they were tested, refined, and validated by these leaders and their team members.

The SERVE Team—These were the men and women we originally assembled more than two decades ago to figure out how to accelerate leadership development at Chick-fil-A—Lee Burn, Mark Conklin, Cynthia Cornog, Lance Lanier, and Phil Orazi.

Thank you for your insights, diligence, wisdom, discernment, and spirit of collaboration. Your influence continues to grow!

Research—We believe one of the things that sets this work apart is the breadth and depth of the research our findings were based upon. Although we had many partners over the years, three distinguished themselves. Mike Fleming and his team from Prophet, Michael Barry and his colleagues from Stanford and Quotient, and Ash Merchant and his associates at AON. These were some of the most impressive teams I've ever worked with. Their diligence and insights were astonishing!

Editorial Team—We have used many, many editors over the years. A few stand out: Katie Dickman, Janice Rutledge, Donna Miller, and Michael Johnson. You folks get the lion's share of credit for the readability of the work I've been a part of for decades. On behalf of our readers, thank you!

Once again, our reviewers provided thoughtful commentary, serious challenge, and tremendous insight as they did the hard and sometimes painful work of reading early drafts. Thanks to Meghan Eliason, Jim Sever, Edgar Brush, Zach Clark, Andrew Cox, Shane Duffey, Jim Fallon, Jennifer Goodwyn, Laci Grigsby, AJ Harper, Justin Miller, Tracy Polite, and Dean Sandbo. Your voices reverberate through this entire book. Thank you!

Global Leaders—Our search for global best practices has allowed us to interact with some of the most phenomenal leaders on the planet. Little of what you've read in this book would exist had we not been so fortunate. Here is a partial list of the organizations we've interacted with:

Accenture	Charles Schwab
Amazon	Chick-fil-A
An Design	Clemson University
Arrow Exterminators	Coca-Cola

Delta
Disney
Dunnhumby
FedEx
Field Museum
Google
Hilton
Joyful Planet
Lee Company
Microsoft
Morning Brew
Netflix
NewSpring Church
Nike
North Illinois Food Bank
NYC Department of
   Education
Oracle
Pixar
Play

Porsche
Professional Children's
   School
Qualtrics
RaceTrac
Ross School of Business
Royal DSM
Salesforce
Snellings Walters Insurance
   Agency
Southwest Airlines
Stanford University
Starbucks
Steelcase
Student Maid
The Edge Group
United Airlines
Vontier
Walmart

Publishing—Thanks to Steve Piersanti and the team from Berrett-Koehler for your belief in the power and potential of our early work. Thanks to Matt Holt and the team from BenBella for helping us get this book and several others out into the world. Both of you have built amazing organizations doing a tremendous amount of good in the world. Thanks for your partnership!

Family and friends—If you've ever published a book, you understand the stress and strain involved. My family and friends have been a constant source of encouragement. My wife, Donna, has been particularly patient over the years. I love you all!

Randy Gravitt—Thanks for being a role model for me and

every leader who knows you. Your passion for the people we serve and the work we do is inspiring. I'm grateful you agreed to coauthor this book with me!

From Randy:

One of my favorite quotes is, "Those who drink the water should never forget those who dug the well." The truth is, I have been drinking from a deep leadership well for decades. So many have encouraged, coached, challenged, mentored, and inspired me to Lead Every Day.

First, I'm grateful to the men and women I had the privilege of serving alongside in multiple organizations over the first 30 years of my career in education and ministry. I learned so much from each of you, and I'm so grateful to have been a small part of such amazing teams and organizations.

I would not be where I am if it were not for a few of my favorite well diggers.

I am so grateful to the first leaders I learned from and admired—my parents. Lee and Patsy Gravitt not only built a great family, they also created businesses, helped build Georgia Power, coached teams, and were incredible leaders in our community. Mom is still leading every day at age 85 and is my hero!

Next, to our entire team of coaches, trainers, and consultants at Lead Every Day. You are the men and women who have helped us serve so many incredible organizations and teams over the past decade-plus. I love you all! A special thanks to Scott Morgan, Stuart Mullins, and Shane Duffey—you all serve so impressively. Well done!

Chuck Cusumano taught me so much in the early days of InteGREAT when it was just the two of us testing much of this content in organizations around the country. Thank you!

Chick-fil-A—I am so blessed to have been chosen as a

strategic partner for such a world-class organization. Training and coaching so many of your executives, restaurant Operators, and team leaders has been one of the great joys of my work life. If I have added a small measure of value, it pales in comparison to the value I have received from your organization.

Thank you to my wife, Laura. You have been exposed to more leadership conversations than you signed up for, but I wouldn't be where I am without you. You truly are the love of my life, and coming home to you is the best part of every day.

Finally, to my coauthor, Mark Miller, is THANK YOU ever really enough? In this case, not even close. But THANK YOU for believing in and asking me to join you on your leadership journey. You have taught me so much about leadership, given me too many opportunities to count, challenged me, coached me, encouraged me, inspired me, and loved me. A man could ask for no better friend!

LEAD EVERY DAY
OPERATING SYSTEM

BECOME A BETTER LEADER

LEARN THE FUNDAMENTALS

CREATE CLARITY

IMPROVE YOUR EFFECTIVENESS

IMPROVE TEAM PERFORMANCE

ATTRACT TOP TALENT

MASTER TEAM BASICS

BUILD GENUINE COMMUNITY

STRENGTHEN YOUR ORGANIZATION

DEVELOP MORE LEADERS

BUILD THE CULTURE

INCREASE ENGAGEMENT

FOCUS ON EXECUTION

TROUBLESHOOTING GUIDE

We decided this book is far too pragmatic to settle for a traditional index. In our on-going quest to create the most practical and helpful content possible, we agreed to build an "Index" based on common pain points, challenges, and questions we hear most often from leaders around the world.

RESOURCES

We trust you found value in what you've just read. Some of you have already begun installing your new Operating System—congratulations! For others, you may need additional information or assistance.

Regardless of what's next for you, our team has created numerous ways to serve you on your journey.

The Lead Every Day Academy. This video-based platform can serve as your virtual mentor as you navigate the Lead Every Day Operating System. We currently have a dozen courses and we'll be adding more in the weeks and months to come. We have plans priced for individuals, teams, and organizations. Learn more at **LeadEveryDayAcademy.com**.

Leadership Coaching and Consulting. Many of you have experienced the life-changing impact of a one-on-one relationship with a coach. We can help you with any facet of the Lead Every Day Operating System and so much more. Over the last decade, we've had the privilege to coach over 2,500 leaders.

Some of you may not be interested in coaching but you may be grappling with a single challenge your team or organization is facing. We offer bespoke consulting engagements based on your needs.

Keynotes and Training. Our team speaks to and trains thousands of leaders every year. Our topics cover the entire spectrum of the content you've just read about. Whether you need inspiration for 10,000, hands-on skills for your leadership team, or anything in between, we would love to explore how we might help you meet your objectives.

The Lead Every Day Show **Podcast.** We produce a podcast for you and leaders around the world. Currently, the show has an audience in more than 150 countries and counting. You can find the show anywhere you download your podcasts.

Other Resources. We have additional books, field guides, assessments, videos, and more to help you Become a Better Leader, Improve Team Performance, and Strengthen Your Organization. You'll find a complete list of resources at **LeadEveryDay.com/ shop**.

For inquiries and access to all resources, go to: **https://leadeveryday .com/the-book/,** *or scan this QR code:*

We look forward to hearing from you!

NOTES

Introduction

1. K. Anders Ericsson and Robert Pool, *Peak: Secrets from the New Science of Expertise* (Houghton Mifflin Harcourt, 2016).
2. K. Anders Ericsson, Michael J. Prietula, and Edward T. Cokely, "The Making of an Expert," *Harvard Business Review*, July 2007, https://hbr.org/2007/07/the-making-of-an-expert.
3. James Clear, *Atomic Habits: An Easy & Proven Way to Build Good Habits & Break Bad Ones* (Avery, 2018).

Update Your Operating System

1. "App Market Statistics," 42matters, accessed September 7, 2024, https://42matters.com/stats.
2. Prophet / Chick-fil-A Leadership POV Quantitative Study, February 2023.
3. Prophet / Chick-fil-A Culture Quantitative Study, May 2021.
4. "Mac OS X Beta Arrives," ABC News, September 13, 2000, https://abcnews.go.com/Technology/story?id=119453&page=2.

BECOME A BETTER LEADER

1. "Extreme Poverty Trend," Gapminder, accessed September 7, 2024, https://www.gapminder.org/data/extreme-poverty-trend.
2. International Labour Organization, *World Social Protection Report 2020–22: Social Protection at the Crossroads—in Pursuit of a Better Future* (Geneva: ILO, 2021).
3. Max Roser and Hannah Ritchie, "Global Child Mortality Timeseries," Our World in Data, accessed September 7, 2024, https://ourworldindata.org/grapher/global-child-mortality-timeseries.
4. World Economic Forum, *Global Gender Gap Report 2020: 100 Years to Pay Equality* (Geneva: World Economic Forum, 2020).
5. Space Operations Command Overview, United States Space Force, 2020,

https://www.spoc.spaceforce.mil/Portals/4/Images/2_Space_Slicky_11x17_
Web_View_reduced.pdf.

Learn the Fundamentals

1. "National Rugby Union Team," New Zealand Rugby History, accessed September 7, 2024, https://nzrugbyhistory.co.nz/national-rugby-union -team/.
2. "All Blacks," All Blacks Official Website, accessed September 7, 2024, https://www.allblacks.com/teams/all-blacks.
3. "Six Sigma Defects Per Million," 6Sigma.us, accessed February 7, 2025, https://www.6sigma.us/process-improvement/six-sigma-defects-per -million/.
4. John Maxwell, "The Law of the Lid," *John Maxwell Blog*, accessed September 7, 2024, https://www.johnmaxwell.com/blog/the-law-of-the-lid/.
5. Deloitte, "Purpose-Driven Companies: Honing a Competitive Edge in 2020," Deloitte Insights, accessed October 25, 2024, https://www2.deloitte .com/us/en/insights/topics/marketing-and-sales-operations/global -marketing-trends/2020/purpose-driven-companies.html.
6. Peter Drucker, "The Best Way to Predict the Future Is to Create It," AZQuotes.com, accessed September 7, 2024, https://www.azquotes.com/ quote/81880.
7. Allen P. Siegel, "The Real Story Behind Apple's 'Think Different' Campaign," *Forbes*, December 14, 2011, https://www.forbes.com/sites /onmarketing/2011/12/14/the-real-story-behind-apples-think-different -campaign/.
8. Blake Morgan, "5 Lessons from Disney's Magical Customer Experience," *Forbes*, January 23, 2020, https://www.forbes.com/sites/blakemorgan/2020 /01/23/5-lessons-from-disneys-magical-customer-experience/.
9. IDEO, "IDEO: Design for a Better World," IDEO, accessed September 7, 2024, https://www.ideo.org/.
10. Google, "Our Approach," How Search Works, accessed September 7, 2024, https://www.google.com/search/howsearchworks/our-approach/.
11. TED, "Ideas Change Everything," *TED Blog*, May 15, 2009, https://blog.ted .com/ideas-change-everything/.
12. Netflix, "About Netflix," accessed September 7, 2024, https://about.netflix .com/en.
13. Red Bull, "Company Profile," accessed September 7, 2024, https://www .redbull.com/us-en/energydrink/company-profile.
14. Lead Every Day, "Lead Every Day," accessed September 7, 2024, https:// leadeveryday.com/.

15. Peter Drucker, "Drucker on Mission," The Drucker Institute, accessed February 7, 2025, https://drucker.institute/wp-content/uploads/2018/08/Reading_Drucker-on-Mission.pdf.

16. Mark J. Perry, "Only 52 US Companies Have Been on the Fortune 500 Since 1955, Thanks to the 'Creative Destruction' That Fuels Economic Prosperity," American Enterprise Institute, accessed September 8, 2024, https://www.aei.org/carpe-diem/only-52-us-companies-have-been-on-the-fortune-500-since-1955-thanks-to-the-creative-destruction-that-fuels-economic-prosperity/.

17. "About Us," Eureka! Ranch, accessed September 7, 2024, https://eurekaranch.com/about-us/.

18. History.com Editors, "Secretariat," History, A&E Television Networks, October 22, 2020, https://www.history.com/topics/sports/secretariat.

19. Ibid.

Create Clarity

1. J. Pryce-Jones, *Happiness at Work: Maximizing Your Psychological Capital for Success* (Wiley Blackwell, 2010), https://doi.org/10.1002/9780470666845.

2. North Point Community Church, "Clarity," Leading Through, accessed September 7, 2024, https://northpoint.org/messages/leading-through/clarity.

3. Kitzu, "Study Highlights Strategies for Achieving Goals," Kitzu, accessed October 25, 2024, https://kitzu.org/study-highlights-strategies-for-achieving-goals/.

4. NASA, "Mars Polar Lander / Deep Space 2," NASA Science, accessed September 7, 2024, https://science.nasa.gov/mission/mars-polar-lander-deep-space-2/.

5. Ibid.

Improve Your Effectiveness

1. Peter F. Drucker, *The Effective Executive* (Harper & Row, 1967).

2. Hermann Plocher, "Hitler Versus His Generals in the West," *Proceedings* 82, no. 12 (December 1956): 1321–33, https://www.usni.org/magazines/proceedings/1956/december/hitler-versus-his-generals-west.

3. "One Study Showed 39% of CEOs Have an Outside Coach and 60% of Growth-Stage CEOs Have a Coach," Upcoach website, June 17, 2022.

4. "The ROI of Executive Coaching," American University, accessed December 3, 2024, https://www.american.edu/provost/ogps/executive-education/executive-coaching/roi-of-executive-coaching.cfm.

5. Michael E. Porter and Nitin Nohria, "How CEOs Manage Time," *Harvard Business Review*, July–August 2018.
6. Howard Gardner, *Leading Minds: An Anatomy of Leadership* (New York: Basic Books, 1995).
7. Joshua Rosenbloom and Stephen Bates, "Kennedy and the Bay of Pigs," Harvard Kennedy School Case Program, January 1, 1998, https://case.hks .harvard.edu/kennedy-and-the-bay-of-pigs/.
8. Ibid.
9. Prophet / Chick-fil-A Change Quantitative Study, March 2022.
10. Interview with the author, 2022.

IMPROVE TEAM PERFORMANCE

1. "Six Sigma Defects per Million," 6Sigma.us, accessed September 7, 2024, https://www.6sigma.us/process-improvement/ six-sigma-defects-per-million.

Attract Top Talent

1. Mark Miller, *Talent Magnet: How to Attract and Keep the Best People* (Berrett-Koehler, 2018).
2. Marshall Goldsmith, *What Got You Here Won't Get You There: How Successful People Become Even More Successful* (Hyperion, 2007).
3. Chris McChesney, *The Four Disciplines of Execution: Achieving Your Wildly Important Goals* (Free Press, 2012).
4. Colorado State University Alumni Association, "Being Held Accountable for Your Goals," AlumLine, accessed February 7, 2025, https://alumline .source.colostate.edu/being-held-accountable-for-your-goals/.
5. Amy Gallo, "What High Performers Want at Work," *Harvard Business Review*, November 6, 2014, https://hbr.org/2014/11/what-high-performers -want-at-work.
6. Kim Parker and Juliana Menasce Horowitz, "Majority of Workers Who Quit a Job in 2021 Cite Low Pay, No Opportunities for Advancement, Feeling Disrespected," Pew Research Center, March 9, 2022, https://www .pewresearch.org/short-reads/2022/03/09/majority-of-workers-who-quit-a -job-in-2021-cite-low-pay-no-opportunities-for-advancement-feeling -disrespected/.
7. Plato, *The Republic*, trans. Paul Shorey (Harvard University Press, 1935), Book VIII.
8. Gallup, "The One Employee Question Leaders Can't Afford to Ignore," Gallup Workplace, accessed September 7, 2024, https://www.gallup.com/ workplace/267014/one-employee-question-leaders-afford-ignore.aspx.

9. Factorial, "The Rule of 7 in Marketing," Factorial HR, accessed September 8, 2024, https://factorialhr.com/blog/the-rule-of-7/.
10. Steven Hankin, "The War for Talent," McKinsey & Company, 1997.
11. Elizabeth Davidson and Rob Kaplan, "How an Accounting Firm Convinced Its Employees They Could Change the World," *Harvard Business Review*, October 13, 2015, https://hbr.org/2015/10/how-an-accounting-firm-convinced-its-employees-they-could-change-the-world.
12. Ibid.
13. Ibid.

Master Team Basics

1. Jon R. Katzenbach and Douglas K. Smith, *The Wisdom of Teams: Creating the High-Performance Organization* (HarperBusiness, 1993).
2. Atlassian, "Workplace Woes: Meetings," accessed October 25, 2024, https://www.atlassian.com/blog/workplace-woes-meetings.
3. Mark McKergow and Paul Z. Jackson, *The Solutions Focus: Making Coaching and Change SIMPLE* (Nicholas Brealey Publishing, 2002).

Build Genuine Community

1. Mark Cartwright, "Thermopylae," World History Encyclopedia. Last modified April 17, 2013, https://www.worldhistory.org/thermopylae/.
2. Ibid.
3. Ibid.
4. Steven Pressfield, *Gates of Fire: An Epic Novel of the Battle of Thermopylae* (New York: Doubleday, 1998).
5. Jon R. Katzenbach and Douglas K. Smith, *The Wisdom of Teams: Creating the High-Performance Organization* (HarperBusiness, 1993).
6. Rudy Giuliani, *Leadership* (Hyperion, 2002).
7. Bill Bender, "10 Ridiculous Stats That Define '85 Bears," *Sporting News*, January 23, 2020, https://www.sportingnews.com/us/nfl/news/1985-bears-stats-espn-30-for-30-video-highlights-history-super-bowl/nea423prcpwv1xf9ec0mur1vk.
8. "1985 Chicago Bears Season," Wikipedia, the Free Encyclopedia, last modified August 28, 2023, https://en.wikipedia.org/wiki/1985_Chicago_Bears_season.

STRENGTHEN YOUR ORGANIZATION

1. ADP Research Institute, *Evolution of Work 2.0: The Changing Nature of the Global Workforce*, July 2018, https://www.adpresearch.com/wp-content/uploads/2020/07/R0101_0718_v2_GE_ResearchReport.pdf.

Develop More Leaders

1. Prophet / Chick-fil-A Leadership POV Quantitative Study, February 2023.
2. 49ers.com, "A Look into the History and Diversity of Bill Walsh's Coaching Tree," San Francisco 49ers, March 9, 2021, https://www.49ers.com/news /a-look-into-the-history-and-diversity-of-bill-walsh-s-coaching-tree.
3. Prophet / Chick-fil-A Leadership POV Quantitative Study, February 2023.
4. ESPN, "Cardinals vs. Braves—Game Summary—October 9, 2019," ESPN, October 9, 2019, https://www.espn.com/mlb/game/_/gameId/401169090/ cardinals-braves.
5. Johnson & Johnson Careers, "Aligning Your Work with Long-Term Career Goals: 4 Tips from Our Talent Experts," Johnson & Johnson, accessed October 25, 2024, https://www.careers.jnj.com/careers/aligning-your-work -with-long-term-career-goals-4-tips-from-our-talent-experts.
6. Zavvy, "Employee Development at Google: Strategies for Success in L&D," Zavvy, accessed October 24, 2024, https://www.zavvy.io/hr-examples/ employee-development-at-google.

Build the Culture

1. Prophet / Chick-fil-A Culture Quantitative Study, May 2021.
2. Ibid.
3. Brent Gleeson, "9 Navy SEAL Sayings That Will Improve Your Organization's Ability to Lead Change," *Forbes*, July 23, 2018, https://www .forbes.com/sites/brentgleeson/2018/07/23/9-navy-seal-sayings-that-will -improve-your-organizations-ability-to-lead-change/?sh=1b0a410864d4.
4. Ibid.
5. NASA, "Apollo 11 Mission Overview," NASA History, accessed September 8, 2024, https://www.nasa.gov/history/apollo-11-mission-overview/.
6. "United Airlines: Grounded," Ethics Unwrapped, McCombs School of Business, University of Texas at Austin, accessed October 25, 2024, https:// ethicsunwrapped.utexas.edu/video/united-airlines-grounded.
7. Lewis Lazare, "United Airlines Has a Plan to Be the 'Most Caring' Airline," *Chicago Business Journal*, January 24, 2018, https://www.bizjournals.com/ chicago/news/2018/01/24/united-airlines-has-plan-to-be-the-most-caring .html.
8. Mark Miller, *Culture Rules* (Matt Holt, 2023).

Increase Engagement

1. Gallup, "How to Improve Employee Engagement in the Workplace," Gallup, accessed September 7, 2024, https://www.gallup.com/workplace /285674/improve-employee-engagement-workplace.aspx.

2.   Ibid.
3.   "McCormick & Company," Wikipedia, the Free Encyclopedia. Last modified August 26, 2023, https://en.wikipedia.org/wiki/McCormick_%26_Company.
4.   "Understanding Taylorism: The History of Scientific Management Theory," MasterClass, accessed September 8, 2024, https://www.masterclass.com/articles/understanding-taylorism-the-history-of-scientific-management-theory.
5.   John T. Landry, "HBR Lives Where Taylorism Died," *Harvard Business Review*, November 19, 2012, https://hbr.org/2012/11/hbr-lives-where-taylorism-died.
6.   Starbucks Coffee Company, "Howard Behar," Starbucks Archive, accessed September 8, 2024, https://archive.starbucks.com/record/howard-behar.
7.   History.com Editors, "Renaissance," History, updated November 12, 2009, accessed September 8, 2024, https://www.history.com/topics/renaissance/renaissance.
8.   Ibid.
9.   National Gallery, "Andrea del Verrocchio," The National Gallery, accessed September 8, 2024, https://www.nationalgallery.org.uk/artists/andrea-del-verrocchio.
10. Ibid.
11. Jonathan Jones, "The Myth of Michelangelo," *The Guardian*, June 7, 2003, https://www.theguardian.com/culture/2003/jun/07/art.

Focus on Execution

1.   SAGE Research Methods Community, "Space Between Stimulus and Response: Creating Critical Research Paradises," Research Methods Community blog, accessed February 7, 2025.

ABOUT THE AUTHORS

Mark Miller is a seasoned business leader, a *Wall Street Journal* and international best-selling author, and a dynamic communicator. He also worked for one of the world's great organizations for almost 45 years.

After a short stint in a local Chick-fil-A restaurant, Mark joined the corporate staff working in the warehouse and mail room as the organization's 16th employee. During his career, he provided leadership for Corporate Communications, Field Operations, Training & Development, Quality and Customer Satisfaction, and Leadership Development.

Mark and his team invested a quarter century and millions of dollars researching and validating ideas to help organizations grow their leaders and improve performance. This work is reflected in a dozen globally acclaimed books. Today, Mark's books can be found in 32 languages around the world—more than 1.5 million copies in print.

An avid photographer, Mark has traveled to some of the world's most difficult-to-reach destinations on all seven continents. He has photographed silverback gorillas in the jungles of Rwanda, icebergs in Antarctica, Nepalese culture at Everest Base Camp, the grandeur of Patagonia, and more.

Mark is married to Donna, his high school sweetheart; they have two sons, Justin and David. Justin and his wife, Lindsay, have three children, Addie, Logan, and Finn. If you ever meet Mark in person, he'll be glad to show you pictures of the kids!

Randy Gravitt is a best-selling author, speaker, and executive coach who encourages leaders to reach their potential.

He started his career in education, spending a decade investing in students and building championship teams in basketball, football, and soccer. Randy then spent nearly two decades helping lead one of the largest churches in the Atlanta area.

In 2014, Randy founded InteGREAT Leadership, building a team of talented coaches, trainers, and consultants who work with high performance leaders, teams, and organizations around the world. In 2024, Randy and Mark teamed up to create Lead Every Day.

As a speaker, Randy delivers keynotes on the topics of culture, team building, and organizational effectiveness. His clients include multi-billion-dollar organizations, including Chick-fil-A, Inc. He has also served as a leadership coach for the Pittsburgh Pirates and the Buffalo Bills.

Randy's previous books include *Winning Begins at Home*, *Finding Your Way*, and *Unstuck*. Randy and Mark's podcast, *The Lead Every Day Show*, is listened to by leaders worldwide from more than 150 countries.

Randy has been married to his wife, Laura, for 38 years. They live in Sharpsburg, Georgia, where they raised four daughters: Hannah, Sarah, Rebekah, and Katherine . . . Girl-dad! He loves being a father-in-law to Trevor, Bryan, Alex, and Airrion, and Ran-Dad to his nine grandchildren: Simon, Isaiah, Micah, Zeke, Scarlett, Millie, Natalia, Jasmine, and a baby girl on the way. Outside of work, Randy enjoys being a scratch golfer, reading, fishing, and sitting on his back porch.

Mark and Randy would love to connect about how they can serve you or your team! Visit their website, **LeadEveryDay.com**, for rich content, free resources, links to their social channels, and more.